(IN)FORMAL L.A.
THE SPACE OF POLITICS

Edited by Victor J. Jones

eVolo

CONTENTS

INTRODUCTION
Victor J. Jones

"Los Angeles is just New York lying down."
—Quentin Crisp

(IN)formal L.A.

Throughout much of Los Angeles' history, the western outpost has been dubbed wild. The sprawling metropolis is cobbled together by individualistic ideas and fierce land speculation. Unlike the habitual gridiron of Manhattan or the strict radial plans of Chicago and Washington, D.C., Los Angeles is a collage of fractious land titles derived from early farm settlements and ranches cradled in a five-hundred-square-mile sun drenched basin. Though the infinite patchwork of subdivisions and development tracts are best seen from above, their patterns belie the subtle ambiguities revealed at close range. Within the endless sprawl and spontaneous urbanism reside flurries of uncodified spatial configurations. No high-definition map or satellite image can accurately trace the mega-city's off-the-record events and ad hoc social formations. As inconspicuous acts are masked behind the restrained façades of New York skyscrapers, Los Angeles' intricate spatial logic is concealed by its laissez faire urban formation. *(IN)formal L.A.* embraces the quirky, celebrates the open ended, and embellishes the up close to expose the complex organization of activities and spaces within this unique urban network.

The Space of Politics

It is impossible to discuss the informal without contemplating the interplay between space and politics. Space is a function of politics. It is the physical evidence of humankind's tireless will to describe and define territories at every scale. In his chapter on "The State and the Individual," Aristotle characterizes politics as the natural outcome of human interaction within the city:

> It follows that the state belongs to the class of objects which exist by nature, and that man is by nature a political animal.[1]

1 Aristotle, *The Politics*, trans. T. A. Sinclair, rev. edition, Trevor J. Saunders (London and New York: Penguin Classics, 1981), 1253a1, 59.

Simultaneously, classical theorists thought of buildings as small cities and of cities as large buildings, with all parts working interdependently and design integral to thinking at every scale. But that legibility has been obscured, as human experience and territory are no longer defined in such finite terms. The informal dynamics of Los Angeles, as they are influenced and shaped by politics, are one such example.

The idea for the book originates from a workshop, (IN)formal L.A.—The Space of Politics, held on August 24–31, 2011. The University of Southern California School of Architecture hosted the event in collaboration with Urban States. The initiative was conceived by visiting professor Stefano de Martino to promote, test, and define converging fields of research and criticism within urban discourse. Our shared interests led Stefano and me to organize the event, which gathered architects, critics, scholars, and students to explore urban spaces ranging from the ultra informal to the highly established and codified. The book offers an opportunity to cultivate an expanded awareness of how politics operate integrally in the spatial affairs of Los Angeles. Here, we observe not an isolated field of operations, but forces that influence spatial constructs of all types.

Departing from a positivist view of Los Angeles as a cluster of urban ecologies freely navigated by cars, highways and wide boulevards as well as dodging the dominant "rules" of the design disciplines, this book aims to redress existing assumptions and stimulate fresh thinking about Los Angeles. To this end, I have compiled eight relevant essays, many by authors who were workshop participants. The first essay was originally printed in 1990. Its sagacious message underpins all subsequent topics.. The material draws another image of the city to interrogate how institutions and people negotiate space. Collectively, the essays, Studio Brief, the students' images from the Pinup and the panel discussion all propose alternative modes of engagement—observation over conjecture, participation over formalism, and non-consensual opportunism over status-quo practices. By formalizing these insights in one publication, I hope to encourage discursive processes traditionally at the margins of architectural discourse.

As we continue in the not-so-new millennium, we need a different route. These field notes, however incomplete, aim to trace an alternative path to productively challenge the institutions and social structures that define civic livelihood.

> Architects have eagerly responded to the call of governments or major private corporations to revamp large areas of cities. Whether architects manage to stay abreast of the broad social and economic forces that underlie changes in the workplace and in the configuration of cities is quite another matter.[2]

This assessment clearly articulates what is at stake. In an era when conventional architectural practices account for only a small percentage of the built environment, does architecture still deliver any "real" value to the human experience? How architectural education and practice can maintain cultural relevance is a critical question.

2 Diane Ghirardo, *Architecture After Modernism* (New York: Thames & Hudson, 1996), 171.

INVISIBLE ACROPOLIS

Diane Ghirardo

Is it possible for architecture to distinguish itself from the institutional aims and philosophies of the patron, those that are its *raison d'être*? More importantly, should it? The Getty Trust's institutional imperatives are cloaked in the gauzy trappings of impeccable and unquestioned cultural and economic verities, so that it constantly engages in an elaborate game of transparency and opacity, apparent openness and adroit concealment. Richard Meier, faced with the task of designing the Getty Trust's new centre for its seven operating programs, produced a project that exposes the modalities of this game with almost too literal but still unerring clarity.

With an endowment of several billion dollars, the proceeds of which must be spent for "the diffusion of artistic and general knowledge," in the 1980s the J. Paul Getty Trust (known as "the Trust" or "the Getty" to intimates, much as another tycoon, Donald Trump, is known as "the Donald") rapidly became the top player in the international art game. Beyond its striking ability to pay unheard of sums for works of art (an estimated $57 million doled out for Vincent Van Gogh's *Irises* in March 1990), the Trust has also moved aggressively into grant-making to institutions, individuals and publications: into document, archive and book collecting; into art education and art information—in short, into nearly every area of connoisseurship and academic pedagogy in the arts. The first of several conflicting tendencies with which the Getty is riven emerge here, for despite embracing the arts, the focus is always Classical and post-Classical Western European art up to 1900, effectively ignoring everything else.

Until Meier's 24-acre complex is completed in 1995, the Trust conducts its wide-ranging activities from skyscraper towers built with Mellon money in Century City. Here, on the back lots of the Twentieth Century Fox studios (the preferred destination of white flight from downtown Los Angeles following the Watts riots in 1965), the fiction of a white society fashioned by investment companies, brokerage and law firms, insurance companies and mortgage bankers stands in counterpoint to the old Hollywood fictions once cranked out in celluloid on the same site. As the corporate art behemoth par excellence, the Trust, with a board of trustees based largely in that hard world of corporate deal making, has been virtually indistinguishable from its more explicitly corporate neighbors.

Moving to a hilltop site in the Santa Monica Mountains manifests a variation on the same theme as embodied in Century City: the fantasy of a world apart from the real world, but here one which is dedicated to the higher things of life—the arts—which remain uncontaminated by the mundane preoccupations of the city at its feet. Not surprisingly, these two informing motifs at times conflict with one another, but the differences are more apparent than real, since in the end they converge on the most basic assumptions and goals.

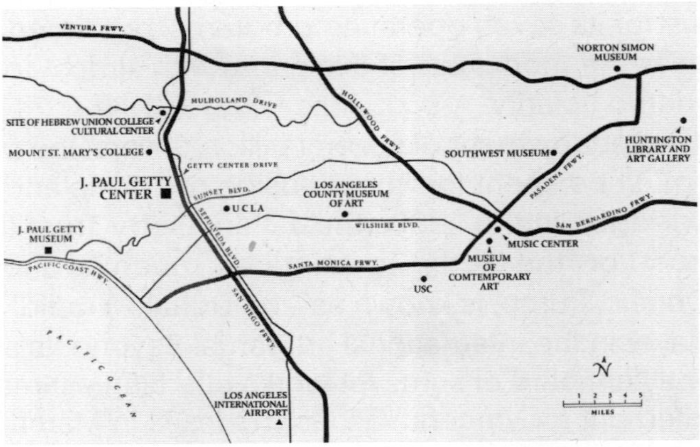

The Getty's own location plan reveals a vision of culture in Los Angeles that consists of a few universities and art museums, with a yawning gap south of the 10 freeway.

Despite an administrative structure, personnel, and board of trustees—not to mention income—that originated overwhelmingly in the boardrooms of corporate America, the Getty harbors quite a different view of itself. Its schematic map of Los Angeles offers a telling indication of this world view, for just as late medieval cartographers identified cities solely by their religious structures and monuments, to the Getty, Los Angeles consists of three or four universities and a few arts institutions. Nowhere does this view emerge with greater clarity than in the choice of the site itself, a secluded spot high atop the Santa Monica mountains overlooking but decidedly remote from Los Angeles: the Trust summarily dismissed sites that would have immersed it in the city. The parking facility at the foot of the hills (mandated by neighbors anxious to preserve their pristine privacy) and public access to the Getty complex only by means of an automated tram system drive home the exclusivity and remoteness with unyielding precision.

But the Getty's mission to engage in the diffusion of art summons other objectives. At least a third of Meier's project is devoted to the museum for collections of pre-twentieth-century Western European paintings, drawings, sculpture, illuminated manuscripts, furniture, decorative arts and photography. All of these share a public destination, along with the associated cafes and gift shops which are standard fare for today's musums. Of the Trust's seven operating programs, only the museum is public in nature; the others are private.

Charged with articulating these dual impulses, Meier made several key moves. The buildings line up on two axes with an approximately 22.5-degree displacement, with the public building, the museum, along one axis, and the non-public buildings straddling the other. Following the tram ride, visitors emerge to face the museum's rotunda, while the Trust and other programs are set slightly back to the left and the scholar's center, archives and library sink one level below grade to the right. Meier emphasizes the public goals of the museum by distributing the gallery and related spaces in a series of pavilions extending out from the rotunda, with temporary exhibitions housed in rotated cubes and permanent ones in the axially aligned pavilions. Likewise, traffic patterns through the museum allow but do not require movement inside and outside and between different levels depending upon climate and preference.

The relative openness and spaciousness of the museum contrasts with the tightly circular footprint of the Getty Center, the art think tank where visiting scholars, library and archives are decidedly not open to the public. Placement on the site and circular form emphasize the private, withdrawn character of the activities within. The private buildings to be clad in sandblasted stainless-steel panels thus flank stone-clad museum buildings, with skylights and few modest openings for fenestration. The exterior therefore delicately balances a serene timelessness and an austere modernity. The interiors promise to be a quite different story. Current museum director John Walsh seems to want to recreate aristocratic interiors, with high wainscoting and flocked wallpaper, in which to display the art, reminding the cultural literati of the elite origins of these displays.

Such a gesture is by no means out of character. In its study, collection and display, the Getty encapsulates the history of bourgeois art within its institutional confines: the passage from an exclusive diversion of the idle aristocracy, accessible to but a few, to its bourgeois appropriation and mass dissemination. The presupposition of a necessary economic surplus, which freed the individual from a daily struggle for existence, gave art its aristocratic status and made it desirable as a measure of status: to collect, commission and display art assumed such freedom. Precisely the uselessness—the idle luxury of the rich—of art and of the aesthetic appreciation associated with it (by contrast with the bourgeois world of production) came to constitute one of its most compelling emblems of high status. With the museum, the Getty must avoid being impaled on the horns of a dilemma, for if its mission to disseminate Western European culture is successful, if the art is truly popularized beyond its legitimate receivers, the legitimacy of those artifacts as opiates for the elite is challenged. It therefore must poise delicately between making available and constantly elevating and imposing exclusivity on the level of discussion about that culture.

In contemporary society, individuals and institutions are assessed according to their capacity to spend and consume above all else; in this category the Getty wins the highest honors. The Getty manages to accomplish the imperatives of a cultural and economic aristocracy: ratifying an impeccable taste structure, rarifying it constantly out of reach of the masses, and manipulating more economic capital than nearly anyone else. With a staggering fortune at its disposal, the Getty confines its entire collection, academic activities and publications to matters long ago blessed by elites of Western Europe and America as the acme of civilization: the artifacts of Classical and post-Classical Western Europe until 1900. The dominant groups of this dominant culture have fashioned the artistic and cultural production of a tiny fraction of the world into an unquestioned and unquestionable standard of quality against which everything else must be measured. Those who purchase, study or display those artifacts claim the arbitrary authority to exclude or devalue other artifacts, or even to re-appropriate those previously scorned, such as the work of the Impressionists once was. All of these fundamental premises of the Getty make it a very problematic institution indeed.

Culture here is not presented as a terrain contested by classes, ethnic groups or nations, but as already determined, absolute and pure. In this sense the Getty calls to mind Disneyland's fantasy recreation of idealized worlds of the past: Main Street USA, for example, scrubbed clean of poverty, homelessness, class, race or ethnic struggle, and even of labor and industrial production. So too is the art enshrined in institutions such as the Getty effortlessly remote from a world of cares. The negative reference point against which this aesthetic culture defines itself is that which is "popular," "middlebrow," or "lowbrow." Instead of understanding art and culture as a living product of collectivities, of struggles, it is here simply a bourgeois fetish in which the less meaningful the object of artistic attention (i.e. *Irises*), the more valuable the work ($57 million), and the greater the emphasis on formal qualities as the measure of the art to the exclusion of others. Although the Getty is not responsible for formulating these attitudes toward a certain class of artifacts, it is responsible for promulgating them: one could have wished for an engaged institution rather than a detached one, one which problematized the notion of culture or art. Given the hegemony of this perspective, it is considered barbaric to ask how such art enriches or improves, for it is one thing to study and appreciate artifacts of the past, and quite another to fetishize them.

In the end, despite moves that subtly attenuate the tension between conflicting impulses, the weight of the institution proves too much even for Meier. The art to be studied and exhibited here, while open to the masses, is clearly destined for what is held to be a specially gifted minority whose aesthetic sense or scholarly acumen distinguishes them from the rest of the world, which, by implication, is how things ought to be. By its very definition, the museum in general neutralizes and decontextualizes artifacts, thereby institutionalizing only one possible attitude, the aesthetic, and privileging form and the detached gaze of the aesthete over everything else. The architecture that makes this possible cannot help but be complicit in the enterprise as a whole. It appears that Meier's project for the Getty will enhance this privileged status of the work of art of Western Europe; although from many sight lines the Getty Center will be invisible, it remains an acropolis for white, Western European culture transplanted to the shores of the Pacific.

Originally published in *Architectural Review* (June 1990).

Since this article appeared in 1990, the architect introduced some changes into the design of the Getty Center, and following the opening in 1994, the institution began to engage in outreach to the local community in a number of ways. It also undertook conservation and other projects in parts of the world not in the pre-1900 Western European orbit. These changes somewhat modify the critique advanced in this article, but not entirely.

BUNDLE OF RIGHTS
Roger Sherman

If entitlements define the legal and spatial interface between a given landowner and the public at large, then the relationship amongst those owning rights by title to a property is outlined by what is referred to as a bundle of rights. Almost from its inception, American land-use law has recognized the concept of ownership with permission, which permits the rights to a given piece of land to extend to more than one party. In fact, it actually assumes a lack of unity between interests vested in a certain property, the intent being to implicitly undermine the accumulation of power through land by dissolving ownership into a complex arrangement accounting for several interested constituents.[1] Termed *rights in the land of another,* these include utility easements, fire rights-of-way, and existing but un-sanctioned site uses, to name a few.[2] As a result, property in many ways resembles a virtual political economy in microcosm, comprised of both competing and cooperating rights holders. These interests—whose influence takes the form of rights, powers, privileges, immunities, and restrictions—range in proximity from local to global. Because each has the right to influence what happens there, their individual motives and collective interaction have as much or more influence on what happens on a given piece of real estate as the physical circumstances of the place or, for that matter, the zoning.

The fact that the law allows for and in fact encourages numerous exceptions to exclusive ownership of land bears important implications for architects. Not the least of these has to do with challenging and even destabilizing the traditional model of architecture patronage, in particular the singularity of the client entity and the concomitant actions and decisions it makes with regard to its property, which the law leaves open to challenge by any party whose rights are (or are likely to be) affected. The logic of American land-use and real estate law suggests a more multifaceted model, wherein the architect is required to act as something of an interlocutor, using the design process as a means of working out differences between entitled and tacit interests. The design itself becomes a framework that visualizes the terms of engagement between parties,

1 David Harvey, *The Condition of Postmodernity: An Enquiry into the Origins of Cultural Change* (Oxford, England: Blackwell, 1990), 93.

2 Ibid., 90–91.

both reflecting the state of their negotiation up to that point and shaping their dealings moving forward.

The bundle of rights is broken into parts, differing in degree of access and permanence; these include *profits a prendre, easements,* and *servitude*. All take preference over the possession (ownership) of the land itself. The result is that relationships between parties on a given lot are far more intertwined, complex, and even messy than either the zoning code or tax assessor's map might suggest. Profit a prendre, the most passive of rights, provides for the holder to profit from or enjoy the resources or products from another's property but falls short of allowing for actual occupation. An example would be the right to harvest the fruit falling into one's own yard from a tree standing in an adjacent property; another, negative form would be a situation in which a landowner is prevented from building on his own property in such a way as to obscure an adjacent owner's legally secured sight line. The easement relieves the owner of exclusive rights to his land. The law terms this type of right, one that exists without visible delineation, a *privilege*. The privilege comes in positive and negative forms. The latter is imposed to restrain an owner from using his own land in certain ways. But most easements are of the former type, which specifically provides for physical access, as in the case of utility companies. Like the easement, the servitude entitles the zer's property for his or her own purposes, but unlike the privilege, it may be physically delineated.

The strip commercial center at the corner of Woodman and Ventura Boulevards in the San Fernando Valley illustrates the complexity that these arrangements can produce. Both formal and informal, direct and more tacit, they result in an intricate set of spatial and material relationships between the parties that are present on the lot (figures 1 and 2). These include Orange Delite, whose concession sits on the corner; Outdoor Systems, whose billboard hovers immediately behind it; La Boutique Cleaners, along the rear of the parcel; and a tropical fish store, which actually sits on the property adjacent but asserts a strong visual presence via the party wall that fronts upon and is shared with the property discussed here. Differing degrees and mediums of control or influence are exercised by each of the rights holders (figure 3). In the case of the juice bar, a stand of orange trees is employed to screen its rear service area; their fragrance extends the aura of its brand across the adjacent parking area. In an enactment

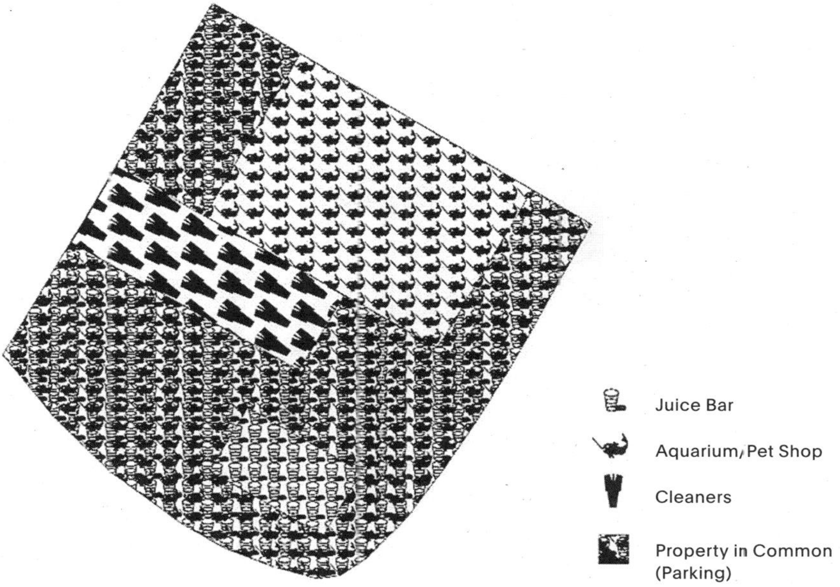

Figure 1 Land use, shared and exclusive, for Woodman and Ventura Boulevards in Van Nuys. Tenant spaces are sub-territories within the larger no-man's-land of asphalt (parking lot).

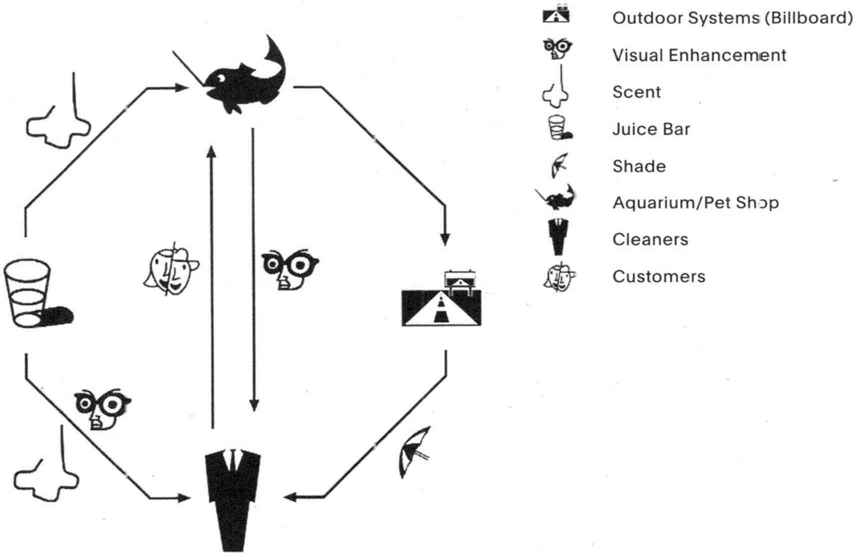

Figure 2 Multilateral exchange diagram for Woodman and Ventura Boulevards, Van Nuys.

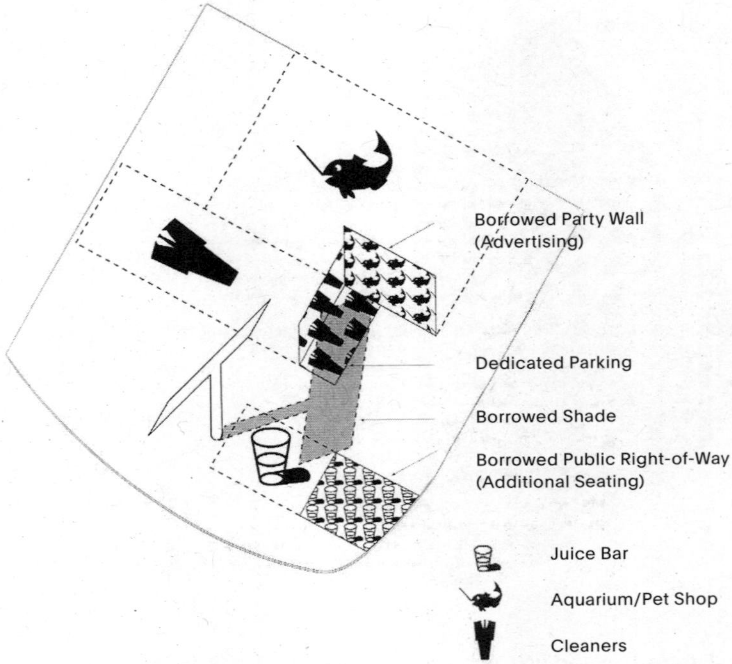

Figure 3 Extended benefits and visibility at Woodman and Ventura Boulevards.

of profits a prendre, its oranges are offered in a bowl on the cleaner's sales counter for customers. (Lest one consider the latter a mere coincidence, one need only look down the counter in the opposite direction, where a bowl of goldfish sits; it does not take long to guess from where it comes, and the nature of the exchange.) Also offering profits a prendre to the cleaners is Outdoor Systems, whose billboard's shadow creates value for La Boutique's customers, who benefits from parking in the reserved spaces it shades, keeping their cars cool (figure 4).

Opportunistically, the neighboring fish store also has negotiated a visual easement with the property owner in order to take advantage of the sight line that the parking lot allows to the store's party wall, on which it advertises itself (figure 5). This visibility comes with a price tag that the property owner understands only too well and is the reason that he welcomes the visual intrusion, as he also does on the case of the billboard, which has also been granted an easement. This differs from the servitude belonging to the juice bar, which enhances the latter's visibility and service capacity by allowing it to extend across the sidewalk, annexing a portion of the right-of-way.

Figures 4 and 5 Woodman and Ventura Boulevards, Van Nuys, c. 1998. Left: View from street past Orange Delite to pet store party-wall advertisement. Right: View of dry cleaner's parking area flanked by Orange Delite and shaded by billboard.

Though property development is predicated on the fulfillment of a bundle of rights, ultimately what happens on-site is the result of the working out of the independent objectives and influences of the involved parties' varied interests, which are unclear and unpredictable at the outset. By understanding how to harness the self-organized logic of negotiation, architects can realize the potential of bargaining as the basis for a new method of producing urban form.

Originally published in *L.A. Under the Influence: The Hidden Logic of Urban Property* (Minneapolis: University of Minnesota Press, 2009).

INSTRUCTIONS FOR THE RECONSTITUTION OF HISTORICAL SMOG

Marcos Sánchez and Mark Wasiuta with Adam Bandler

Atmospheric Report for Wednesday, September 14, 1955
High: 93 degrees F
Ozone Peak: .64 parts per million
Inversion lid at 1000 feet
First Stage Smog Alert

Reversibility

Ozone. Carbon monoxide. Nitrogen oxides. Sulphur dioxide. Hydrocarbons. Recorded daily since 1945, the air data of Los Angeles is a vast, intricate archive of pollutants, particulates, and atmospheric signals. Compiling decades of chemical miasmas and years of successive microscopic accumulation, the city's air records demonstrate a peculiar mediatic reversibility. Read not as result, residue, or informational remainder but rather as a detailed schedule of materials and quantities, Los Angeles' air archives supply precise ingredients for the reconstitution of historically accurate smog.

Molecular History

An indistinct body of volatile ingredients, photochemical smog fluctuates in toxicity, visual intensity, and internal composition. Aerosol chemical concentrations respond to sunlight intensity, wind currents, relative humidity, and to the particulates and gases released into the air. Sired by the union of meteorological conditions and industrial activity, smog is born as an articulate medium of historically and geographically specific atmospheric expression. Not only are the features of Los Angeles smog different from smog found in Cairo or Mexico City, the smog of 1955 bears a distinct chemical signature, easily distinguished from one of five, ten, or fifteen years later.

The difference among smog samples is a factor of the technological, economic, and social composition of the city below. Los Angeles Air Pollution Control District (APCD) sampling stations harvested numerous species of particulate material flung into the air during the city's explosive postwar expansion. Fertilizer and soil from San Fernando Valley farming, carbon from diesel ships feeding the city's port, ash from backyard garbage incinerators, synthetic rubber from nylon-belted tires, and concrete dust from freeway construction joined to generate the pollutant patterns of a specific era. As registered in the records of the APCD air-monitoring network, Los Angeles smog delivers a material history of the city at the molecular level.

Air Agency

While the archival record of smog traces the molecular detritus and material emanation from the city, it is also evidence of smog's transformative effects. Photochemical smog is both aerial recipient of suspended surface matter and a reactive force that breeds ever more particulates as it attacks rubber, nylon, and other ubiquitous urban materials. This dynamic and corrosive interaction with the substance of the city distinguishes photochemical smog from 19th century clouds of soot and dust and other periods' airborne contaminants. Through its reactivity, Los Angeles smog became a potent manifestation of novel postwar air ecology. Saturated by supplements and pollutants, Los Angeles' atmosphere in turn became an active protagonist in the city.

During the 1950s this atmospheric feedback enveloped the Los Angeles Basin's air bureaucracy. The formation of new and increasingly powerful agencies such as the APCD signaled the postwar copula of regional administration and city air. Bronchial irritation and chest pain, commonly referred to as "smog syndrome," combined with persistent low-visibility and crop damage to cause an escalating atmospheric anxiety. Armed with observation codes, lab analysis procedures, and a growing archive of air measurements, the administration echoed early modern responses to the "pathogenic city" by positioning municipal government between the urban population and techniques of atmospheric management. Initially produced by the city, smog now participated in the regulation of city life, through the governmental action it compelled.

In a city accustomed to wartime deployments of the civil defense apparatus, the initial engagements between the administration and smog reprised the rhetoric of militarized air space. Now facing pollution, air emergency procedures and the terminology of "smog attacks" aided the growth of an air-sampling network that attempted to track an inscrutable enemy. These airborne threats ultimately became the basis for a new formulation of the city environment that required correspondingly novel forms of information, administration and defense.

Smog Threat

The reconstitution of historical smog expands the object of preservation to include the corrosive air that infiltrated postwar architecture as well as the toxins and chemicals that conditioned the urban ecology of postwar Los Angeles. Conventionally, precisely these caustic agents would be excluded from any preservation project that would seek to isolate, secure, and rescue architecture from Los Angeles' smog effects. Yet the city's spaces, buildings, vision, and urban imaginary have been colored and historically altered by this constant backdrop of iridescent or murky toxicity as much as by other forces. Los Angeles' atmosphere is not only a protean body of polluted air that hovers in the distance; it is also a cultural artifact that permeates the city, its population, and its architecture.

Smog's gases and particulates were engendered by the same manufacturing practices that made building materials widely available. Its ingredients were produced and aerosolized by suburban construction and by the proliferating car ownership that fostered suburban life. Smog is not only the by-product of urban expansion in Southern California but also its inseparable complement.

UNESCO's studies of photochemical smog in Europe consistently focus on the deleterious effects of smog measured through acid rain and the surface degradation of historical monuments. In contrast, Los Angeles is largely free of both rain and stone construction. The city seals itself from smog in the conditioned interiors of automobiles and architecture, protected by their own defensive air systems. The most consequential corrosion associated with smog in Los Angeles is not on architectural surfaces but within the filtering apparatuses, sealants, gaskets and other barriers and technologies of atmospheric isolation. The architecture and filtered environments of Los Angeles are under threat at their edges, seams, and hinges.

2880 Cubic Feet

Guided by the archive's reversibility, the instruction diagram below is divided into two categories. "Record" indicates how air is sampled and its contents analyzed. "Replay" describes how an atmospheric chamber is used to reconstruct photochemical smog from the air analysis.

Via this set of instructions we reproduce air sampled by the APCD Central Station in downtown Los Angeles on September 14, 1955, the date of one of the first massive smog emergencies.

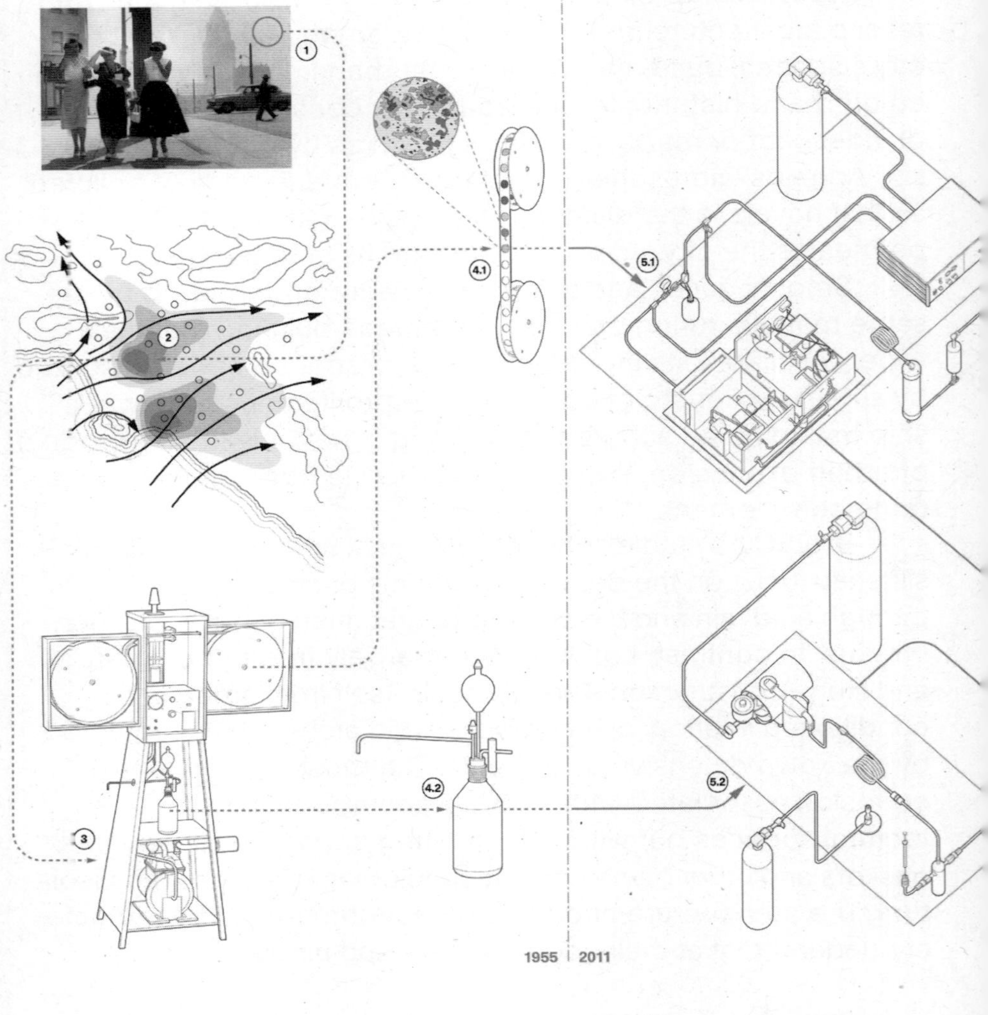

1. Air Condition
Photograph from September 14,1955. Image shows air conditions during a smog alert in downtown Los Angeles near Air Pollution Control District Station 1. Temperature high of 93 degrees Fahrenheit, inversion lid at 1,000 feet.

2. Air Network
Map of the Los Angeles Basin showing typical onshore air movement. By 1955, the APCD network included dozens of sampling stations distributed throughout the basin measuring contaminants, eye irritation, and plant damage. Map indicates APCD Station 1 and other main sampling locations.

3. Air Sampling Station
APCD air sampler used until the early 1960s to collect particulate matter. Over one hour air was drawn through 2 inch filter discs mounted in a "reel-to-reel" belt. At the end of the hour, the belt would advance and the cycle would repeat to produce a continuous material recording. Motors and other equipment were housed within the base of the station, where ambient air samples were drawn into a glass and metal canister for later lab analysis.

4.1. Particulate Sampling
After the filtration phase the disks carried data on pollutant ratios and particulate density, measured in micrograms per cubic meter.

4.2. Hydrocarbon Sampling
Air samples collected at network stations were analyzed using gas chromatographs; this equipment measured hydrocarbons in units of parts per million (PPM).

5.1. Particulate Injection
A graphite aerosol generator is used to produce carbon particles, which are mixed with purified air and injected into the reactor bag. The resulting suspended particulate density follows the 1955 measurements.

5.2 Hydrocarbon Injection
Xylene, a hydrocarbon present in solvents and fuels, was registered across the Los Angeles basin from the 1950s onward. Here, it is vaporized into a stream of molecular nitrogen (N2). The resulting vapor is then injected into the reactor bag. A similar apparatus used for each hydrocarbon results in hydrocarbon concentrations equal to those of the target date.

6. Chamber System Diagram
(A) Components for supplying a continuous flow of purified air to the enclosure around the reactor bag. This prevents outside pollutants from migrating into the bag. (B) Equipment used to supply UV radiation to the bag. The two banks of black lights match the emission spectrum of sunlight between 300 and 450 nm.
(C) Components used to inflate the reactor bag with purified air, and later, to inject a flow of pollutants the bag. A separate system (not shown) samples bag contents to achieve and maintain the require balance of ingredients. (D) Wearing a sealed tran ent helmet, a subject is exposed to the bag cont Viewing a Snellen eye chart, the retinal irritation obscuring of vision associated with the 1955 sm syndrome are manifest.

7. Smog Construction Sequence
A clean air generator fills the FEP- Teflon reactor with purified air; pollutants are then injected thro bag's side ports. Black light arrays irradiate the b aerosol contents with UV light, producing contro specific photochemical reactions. After irradiati reactor's contents match air samples taken on S ber 14, 1955, resulting in a volume of historical a

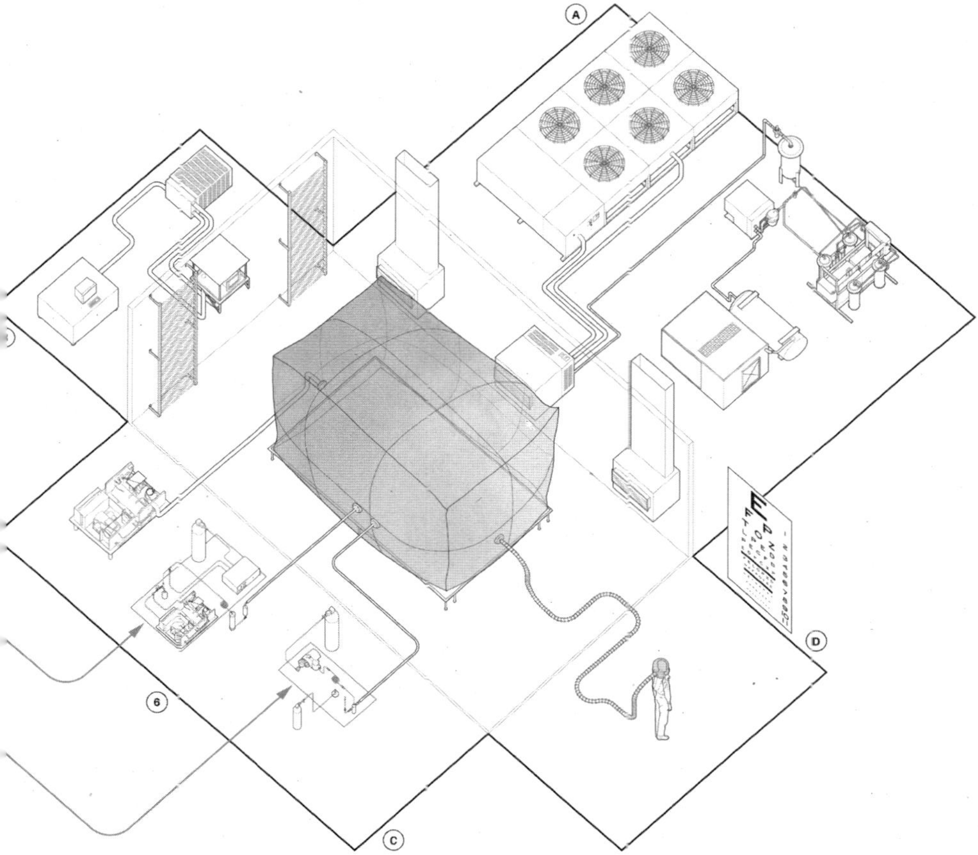
A
6
C
D

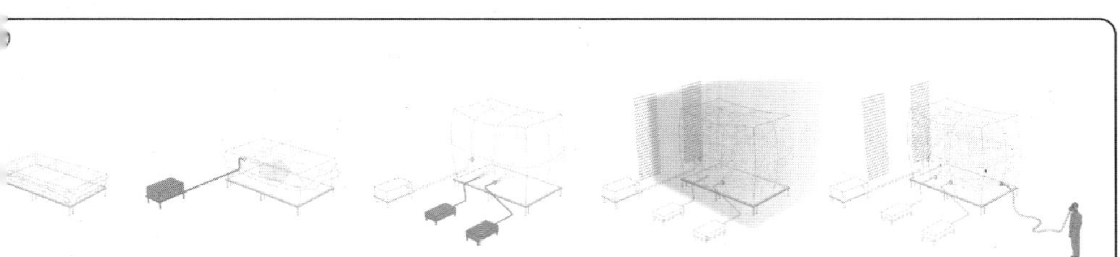

In "Record," the first sequence of steps depicts APCD sampling equipment (ca. 1955) and the pollutant information this technology delivered. Rooftop devices that trapped particulates against a rotating filter measured a first key component of smog, microscopic dust suspended in the air. A second component, the day's combination of pollutant gases, was captured for later analysis in the APCD laboratory, where the agency's personnel recorded levels of hydrocarbons and other airborne compounds. As the APCD expanded in the years after the Second World War, it multiplied sampling locations into a regional network of fixed and mobile air testing stations. The agency's ongoing measurements supplied a data record of pollutants whose combination was specific to the date, season, and meteorological conditions of a precise location within the city.

"Replay," the diagram's second category, shows particulates and gases being assembled and injected into an atmospheric "reactor" alongside a stream of purified air. The chamber and ancillary equipment follow a common design of atmospheric modeling facilities built for the study of aerosol pollutants and photochemical reactions. The primary purpose of the reactor is to hold this mixture aloft while it is lit by an array of fluorescent black lights. In this final phase of smog construction, the chamber's contents are irradiated with ultraviolet light of approximately the same spectrum as sunlight, replicating photochemical reactions that occurred on the day the pollutants were originally recorded. Once the black lights complete their irradiation cycle, the net product of this sequence is 2880 cubic feet of historical smog.

Smog Chroma

While demonstrating the corrosive potency of photochemical smog, the resulting volume of reconstituted historical air does not exhibit the characteristic hydrocarbonate color range associated with the vistas of late Los Angeles summer. Although pollutant concentrations in the air chamber equal those found in archival smog data, aerial light refraction does not successfully scale or compress. The dominant view in the atmospheric laboratory, outside of the short-lived violet glow of the black lights, is the equipment that constructs and supplies the pollutant-air mixture, what Reyner Banham called "environmental provisions."

The relative visibility or invisibility of smog pervades the project of historical reconstitution. Although historical patterns of toxic intensity and visual density correspond only approximately, visual perception is critical to smog's urban identity. Despite its potential visual imperceptibility, the secondary attributes of haze and color are generally Los Angeles smog's most obvious phenomena.

Where the instruction diagram uses color coding as a graphic surrogate for the absent smog chroma, the assembly compensates for the elusive visual features with the attached smog helmet. While the bag's contents are not visible from outside the reactor, they are immediately perceptible from within the breathing apparatus. By exposing the naked eye to the chemical contents, the reconstructed smog's visual evasion is arrested, irradiated, and exposed into an acute optical condition, triggering a form of historic vision. Immersed in smog, the subject registers the aerosol mixture through respiratory distress, chest pain, ocular discharge, and tears, symptoms of the smog syndrome first described in the 1950s. Less an optical illusion than occlusion, the apparatus ultimately induces the perception of blurs, hazes, and the indistinct boundaries of the smog horizon.

Originally published in *PRAXIS: Journal of Writing + Building*, issue 13: Ecologics (March 2012).

YIELD

BOGOTÁ > LOS ANGELES
Rachel Berney

Introduction

Bogotá, Colombia, which completely transformed its urban environment starting in the 1980s, offers a provocative model of development for the city of Los Angeles. What connects the two cities is their shared focus on improving public space and public transport options for their citizens. Since the 2000s, Bogotá has been considered a model of urban development. It re-made itself beginning in the late 1980s into an "everyday city," that is, a city that supports the daily needs of its residents, including the ability to commute comfortably and to have shared spaces in which to relax and to engage with other citizens. These changes came about within the realm of public space.

Los Angeles is now embarking on a similar transformation. City leaders seek to double the miles of public transit rail and number of transit stations, creating the best opportunity in decades to shape the city's urban public realm. Los Angeles is following in Bogotá's footsteps to become an everyday city, yet a key difference between the cities is that while Bogotá focused on reclaiming public space from private interests as a fundamental strategy, in Los Angeles, city government is searching for solutions to revenue deficits by renting public space to private enterprise.

The Strategic Territory of Public Space

History and tradition in Latin America dictate that public space is a normative element of a city's physical structure—from the founding of cities around *plaza mayors* and the creation of neighborhoods surrounding churches and their plazas to *avenidas* that connect different areas of the city. In Latin America, public space also plays a fundamental role in a city's social structure by creating the ability for individuals to interact with friends and strangers, which offers key opportunities to build citizenship.

In the 1980s, civil society in the capital city of Bogotá lay in tatters. Mayors were elected for the first time in the city's history, and they were empowered by the new decentralization of government and the shift in responsibility from the national to the local level. Hoping to revive the historic dual role of public space, city leaders launched urban transformation projects in the 1990s and 2000s that focused on remaking the city and reclaiming public space for the people. Mayoral administrations initiated new policies and built institutions tasked with the creation of lively open space, and they backed up these policies and their associated programs with unique tools.[1]

Bogotano mayors were concerned about the significant inroads that private interests had made into public spaces, such as citizens claiming public space as part of their own private property, fixed-stall markets springing up in plazas, private bus services clogging streets, and mobile vendors using public space for private profit. The mayors reversed these trends and created a clearer demarcation between public and private uses of public space.

Rather than limiting commercial incursions, city leaders in Los Angeles see private enterprise in public space as one solution to the city's financial woes. As taxation reaches a ceiling, local leaders have identified the public realm as a source of revenue. Today, valet companies lease city parking spaces, billboards are located on public lands throughout the city, and cafés lease sidewalk space to extend their dining areas outside. These actions effectively limit public use of public space. Instead, people must pay to enjoy certain services and activities within spaces that they, as citizens, collectively own.

Public space is more peripheral to daily life in Los Angeles than in Bogotá. Population and work centers are spread out across the city and beyond and people frequently commute many miles to and from work each day and spend several hours in the car each week for family, work, and social obligations. By virtue of its size and expansive, freeway-dominated transportation network, the city is fundamentally oriented toward cars rather than pedestrians. Another issue is that Los Angeles' public green spaces range from overused and under-maintained urban neighborhood parks to vast but inaccessible tracts of hillside chaparral. Los Angeles has some remarkable open spaces, but they are not where the majority of Angelinos spend their time. After a long day of work and commuting, most people retreat into their private spaces to rest and relax.

During Bogotá's transformation, city officials greatly increased the amount of accessible public space and declared

1 One of the most interesting of these tools was the creation of the Defensoría del Espacio Publico, a city government body charged with reclaiming, protecting, and managing the city's public space.

that its maintenance would be covered by city budgets, yet it was clear to many even at the time that this would not be possible. [2] Bogotá is challenged, like Los Angeles, by the costs of acquiring, developing, and, especially, maintaining public open space. Increasing public-private partnerships for the support of public open space is a likely solution in both cities. Such partnerships, however, increase the influence of private agendas over public spaces.

Visible Competency as Political Practice

Elected leaders seek to demonstrate "visible competency" through making changes in the city that enhance their legitimacy. In particular, by displaying that they have the ability to plan, design, and implement capital improvement projects in public space and make an impact on people's daily lives, city governments demonstrate competency in a highly visible way. Projects in public space do this by inviting people in to engage with others through formal and informal activities. Over time these projects influence the *spatial logic* of the city—the physical arrangement of components of the built environment in relationship to the political, social, and cultural forces at play. Collectively, they reflect city government legitimacy.

During its period of transformation, Bogotano mayors set out to reinvent civil society by drawing people out of their homes and into public spaces to interact with one another. Bogotanos were encouraged to recreate in the new public spaces, to visit the new cultural institutions that were deliberately located at the nexus of public transit, bike path, and open space opportunities, and to use the new public transport systems that connected areas of very different socioeconomic status with one another. Through public space planning, Bogotá became a *pedagogical city*, with a spatial logic composed of an interrelated network of parks and plazas, cultural institutions such as libraries, *ciclorutas* (bicycle paths), and the TransMilenio Bus Rapid Transit system.

Today, Los Angeles is poised to become the *mobile city*, one connected and networked via public transportation with higher density housing at transit nodes and with opportunities to reweave the urban fabric of the city to incorporate public space. The city is dedicated to building one of the most ambitious light rail and

2 Rachel Berney, "The Pedagogical City: How Bogotá, Colombia, Is Reshaping the Role of Public Space," PhD dissertation, University of California, Berkeley, 2008.

subway systems in the country. The spatial logic is one of massive underground and right-of-way infrastructure investments with key opportunities for the development of public spaces around strategically placed transit stations.

Much public space investment in Los Angeles currently occurs by piggybacking public space projects onto larger capital improvement projects. The lack of open space in the city creates challenges for finding appropriate places in the city to locate new projects. New public space must be wedged into the existing urban fabric by strategic means. These acupunctural inserts, combined with expansive public transit, are the city's best opportunities for expanding the public realm well into the future.

In Bogotá in the 1980s, public resources were used for private gain, socioeconomic differences resulted in tremendously uneven living conditions, and the city fabric had been neglected. It was imperative for local leaders to show a responsibility to their constituents by investing in public works. In Los Angeles, where city government must respond to gridlocked freeways and threadbare or inaccessible green space, it is a similarly crucial time for reinvention and change.

The Everyday City

The advantages for Bogotá and Los Angeles seeking to be everyday cities include city form and function that better support daily activities and projects that demonstrate visible competency. In addition, people going about their business in public open spaces is good for business. Through "everyday urbanism,"[3] the daily material practices of people—life patterns, habits, and decisions—are the definitive shapers of the spaces and relationships around them, and thus become complicit in the political economy of the city. This privileges the spectacle of the everyday.[4] Rather than using grand spectacles, as favored by many city builders and boosters throughout history, in Bogotá, city leaders focused on everyday activities—using the park, riding bikes, and going to the library—to demonstrate the economic and social vitality of their city. Los Angeles is poised to follow suit.

3 See John Chase, Margaret Crawford, and John Kaliski, eds., *Everyday Urbanism* (New York: Monacelli Press, 2008).

4 See Rachel Berney, "Public Space Versus Tableaux: The Contradiction between the Right to the City and Neoliberal Capital in Bogotá, Colombia," in Tony Roshan Samara, Shenjing He and Guo Chen, eds., *Locating Right to the City in the Global South: Transnational Urban Governance and Socio-Spatial Transformations* (New York: Routledge, 2012).

Informality—activities that have historically operated outside of established formal and legal urbanization practices[5] —also plays a role in the everyday city. In Bogotá, to help ensure the success of these spaces of encounter and learning, behavior in public spaces was monitored by civic "agents" —from signage to program leaders and police.[6] Within this process, a practice of everyday urbanism was constructed, yet people engaging in certain types of informal economic activities were penalized. As a result, in Bogotá, a state of *managed informality* was created in which some types of vending were allowed (selling lottery tickets or books, for example) yet other types were not (selling food at street intersections and selling directly from the sidewalk). Informality is seen here as *extra legal,* falling outside of legal processes and actions.[7]

In Los Angeles, informal economic activities appear to be everywhere, from vendors selling bags of fresh-cut fruit along the side of the road to taco stands set up in vacant parking lots. Yet many of these types of activities are no longer informal. Vendors have city permits, event organizers select which food trucks to invite to their events, and shop owners and cafes pay for the use of sidewalk space. These official "invitations" to occupy public space negate informality. The newest and perhaps most interesting example of this is that city planning staff are considering permitting vendors on Metro plazas and in rail stations. While not uncommon in other cities, this represents a reversal of Los Angeles city policy.

Partly because many of Los Angeles' public spaces are not well used, city leaders are embracing the spectacle of the everyday and so-called informal activities to enliven the city. In its own way, Los Angeles is attempting to harness and manage informality. Unlike Bogotá, however, where informality is seen as a threat to the "orderly city," in Los Angeles informality is seen as the vehicle for the "lively city."

In viewing Los Angeles through the lens of Bogotá, the discussion circles back to two key questions: What is the role of public space? And how is the city making use of its

5 Ananya Roy, "Urban Informality: Toward an Epistemology of Planning," *Journal of the American Planning Association* 71:2 (2005): 147.

6 See Rachel Berney, "Pedagogical Urbanism: Creating Citizen Space in Bogotá, Colombia," *Planning Theory* 10:16 (2011): 16–34.

7 This is a reversal of the historical tradition in Latin American cities, where people teach and do business in public space. See Setha Low, *On the Plaza: The Politics of Public Space and Culture* (Austin, TX: University of Texas Press, 2000).

public spaces? In Bogotá, public policy sought to draw people out of private spaces and into public space in an attempt to rebuild camaraderie and, through it, civil society. In Los Angeles, people are invited into public spaces that are made more comfortable and entertaining through the trappings of privatization and commercialization. In the future, Los Angeles may have opportunities to teach its citizens what it means to live in a city with an engaging public realm and ample transit options.

THE STUDIO AND THE CITY: NOTES ON ARCHITECTURAL PEDAGOGY

Kenny Cupers

The pedagogical history of the architecture studio has yet to be written. But one of the things it would likely reveal—apart from an oscillation between the autonomy of the studio as a place of production and its engagement with the dynamics of the built environment at large—is the sheer proliferation of pedagogical approaches over the past decades, from form-generating coding and ecological performance calculation to casting concrete and building emergency shelters. Despite the plethora of experimentation, studio pedagogy today still lacks one crucial dimension: an engagement with the concrete spatial realities of the world around us. In my view, the vitality of architecture—both as a discipline and as a profession—hinges upon this. Even design-build and community-based studios, which often do a terrific job of incorporating experiential learning and social awareness into design research, display little patience with understanding a site prior to the framing device that is design intervention.[1] The fact that this problem can be described in such enormously general terms is only a sign of the poverty that confronts us in thinking through it today.

A principal goal of architectural education should be to enable students to think both analytically and projectively about what surrounds them: the built environment. Rather than accepting it as things that are just "there," architectural pedagogy should encourage students to interrogate how exactly buildings, landscapes, and cities are continuously made and unmade by layers of decisions and the rhythms and contingencies of everyday life. That interrogation of this ongoing process is exactly where the analytical can feed the projective imagination. Beyond authored works of architecture and planners' intentions, the built environment—in its banality as well as its uniqueness—not only tells us something about culture and society, it also helps shape the multiple forces that make up our world. The development of that analytical capacity is, of course, at least partly the job of architectural history. But why leave

1 For an overview of contemporary approaches, see *Design Studio Pedagogy: Horizons for the Future*, ed. Ashraf M. Salama and Nicholas Wilkinson (Gateshead: The Urban International Press, 2007).

what is arguably the discipline's central subject outside of the studio?

To that rhetorical question, Denise Scott Brown, Robert Venturi, and Steven Izenour responded with an unparalleled pedagogical experiment that placed the studio squarely in the city. *Learning from Las Vegas*, the publication that resulted from their studio at Yale in 1968, sparked architectural debates that have in many ways obscured the project's most essential contribution to architecture. In subsequent decades the project has been appreciated less as a pedagogical revolution and a reevaluation of architecture's relationship to the built environment than as a discursive argument in what ultimately turned into the postmodernist embrace of architecture's autonomy. Canonized for the wrong reasons, *Learning from Las Vegas* was only recently hailed for its pedagogy, coinciding with the popularity of the "research studio" in the wake of Rem Koolhaas's *Project on the City* in the late 1990s.[2] But by this time, urban research in the studio amounted to little more than replacing the CAD architect with the Google architect, neither of which took students away from their screens. At times, the boldest arguments about urban life were forged without doing so much as looking out the window of the studio. Research findings ended up—despite best intentions—serving the discipline more than contributing to knowledge about the contemporary city. Up until today, research in the studio threatens to follow this logic when it becomes immediately instrumentalized in the mill of architectural production. In the best cases, studio-based research contributes to a more sophisticated, process-driven design pedagogy, which can encourage students to be more reflexive about what they make and how they can test it. But what does this ultimately mean for our understanding of architecture's role in the world?

Meanwhile, research as a process by which things are examined on their on own terms continues to be absent in many architecture schools. If there is some attention to the analysis of urban form, its myriad consequences on the ground, in the spaces of everyday life are often relegated to the purview of disciplines such as history or social science. When the belief, popular with modernists, that use was a simple consequence

2 See Kazys Varnelis, "Is There Research in the Studio?" *Journal of Architectural Education* 61.1 (2007): 11–14. The theme of the issue is Architectural Design as Research, Scholarship, and Inquiry.

of design became discredited, two parallel yet divorced paths seem to have emerged from the ensuing anxiety. "Architectural phenomenologists" clung to the notion of an authentic first-hand experience of buildings, while "environmental designers" based the future of architecture on the promises of social scientific knowledge. Both ended up offering little toward an understanding of that which "real architects" generally do not design, namely the vast majority of the built environment today. What we need to do instead of reviving these ideologically charged routes of the past is to promote a more pragmatic approach to the pedagogy of the architecture studio.

In his essay *The School and Society*, published in 1900, John Dewey outlined an approach to learning that could be remarkably fruitful for architectural pedagogy today.[3] Dewey advocated an overhaul of what was the dominant view of education in his eyes, namely the idea of students as receptacles for knowledge and teachers as the depositors. Instead of abstract learning, he proposed learning by doing—an idea that at first glance seems nothing more than what has long been the goal of the studio in the pedagogy of architecture. But, rather than seeing this realm as enclosed within itself, the way students sometimes feel behind their computers in their studios, as slaves of a lonely ship, Dewey envisioned an intense relationship between the school and society, in our case, the studio and the city. In his Laboratory School at the University of Chicago,[4] firsthand experience of natural and industrial processes fostered a proactive attitude toward life and learning, a pragmatic approach he believed could overcome the separation between theory and practice. Admittedly, Dewey's vision was squarely rooted in the liberal ideologies of industrial capitalism: education was meant to make that machine run smoothly.

Even though it would be a mistake to transpose his vision directly onto today's situation, some of his ideas are pertinent to the contemporary teaching of architecture. Too often, the intellectual development of architecture students tends to isolate them from the concrete realities around them. For those who conceive of such environments in their studios, it is crucial to complement abstract thinking with an empirical understanding

3 John Dewey, *The School and Society: Being Three Lectures* (Chicago: University of Chicago Press, 1900).

4 See Eugene F. Provenzoi Jr., "History as Experiment: The Role of the Laboratory School in the Development of John Dewey's Philosophy of History," *The History Teacher*, 12.3 (May 1979), 373–82).

of the contradictory qualities of the world around them. More than the ability to solve design problems, studio pedagogy could provide students not just with knowledge or skills, but also with a proactive attitude toward learning that exceeds the bounds of the institution. What is needed, therefore, are technique geared specifically to developing students' sensorial intelligence, their ability to see and understand buildings, landscapes, and cities. This entails not only visual analyses of artistic representations, photographic reportage, architectural drawings, and urban maps and plans in class, but more importantly, firsthand and participant observation techniques enabling students to learn freely and independently. Teaching that reveals how existing accounts and representations of the built environment are themselves normative constructions, often generated in order to advance a particular agenda for change, fosters the analytic thinking needed to make the creative leap into the production of one's own interpretation and the interrogation of one's own predispositions. Criticality and theory are essential components of this endeavor: rather than being mere add-ons, they are embedded in the messiness of the built environment itself. An understanding of the complex relationship between architecture and the built environment at large should be a central part of studio pedagogy because this, more than any other skill, provides students with the agency to position themselves as innovative professionals in the contemporary city.

Editor's Notes on the Studio Brief

The studio brief for (IN)formal L.A.—The Space of Politics naturally finds its "*racines*" in the work of British historian Reyner Banham. In the course of a 1972 residency at the University of Southern California, Banham made the BBC documentary *Reyner Banham Loves Los Angeles*. The film records Banham driving around Los Angeles in a convertible Impala dubbed "Baede-kar."[1] Forty years later, it serves as a conceptual underpinning for this investigative workshop.

At first, the design project for (IN)formal L.A. was an urban archaeological exploration. Students surrendered their design cubicles and their preconceived notions about the city to explore Los Angeles firsthand. With references to Robert Venturi and Denise Scott Brown's *Learning from Las Vegas* and Yoshiharu Tsukamoto and Momoyo Kajima's *Made in Tokyo*,[2] the studio emphasized fieldwork.

Analysis as research became the preeminent design project—a topic Venturi and Scott Brown reluctantly omitted from *Learning from Las Vegas*.[3] Rather than contrive formalistic visions of architecture or conjure improbable spaces from mental images, students went into the city to find tangible points of reference.

The students were apprehensive about the project. There was no program, no specified site, and no indication of a conventional architectural project. They wondered, what do we design? How do we work? To what ends? Usually, students are either so far away from the project site that direct access is untenable or when they are able to visit the site, they possess no tangible ability to articulate or record the nature and qualities of a place. Markus Miessen and Kenny Cupers's message to the students during the week-long workshop was to go out and see—master the skill of observation and develop convincing methods for recording those findings.

1 The reference is to Karl Baedeker, the 19th-century German publisher of authoritative guidebooks to cities.

2 Yoshiharu Tsukamoto and Momoyo Kajima, *Made in Tokyo: Guide Book* (Tokyo: Kajima Institute Publishing, 2001) and Kyoichi Shinada, *Pet Architecture Guide Book*, vol. 2 (Tokyo: World Photo Press, 2002).

3 Denise Scott Brown, "On Formal Analysis as Design," *Research Journal of Architectural Education* 32.4 (May 1979): 8–11. Also mentioned in the original introduction of *Learning from Las Vegas* (Robert Venturi, Denise Scott Brown and Steven Isenour, *Learning from Las Vegas: The Forgotten Symbolism of Architectural Form*, rev. edition [Cambridge, MA: MIT Press, 1977]).

(IN)formal L.A. makes apparent the insufficiency of Google Earth and other satellite mapping devices: the resulting stitched together facsimile is often misleading. Learning to see and record evocative site information firsthand through photography and writing is integral to design understanding. Students must be able to describe an urban environment and to identify and distill the elements that hold design value.

The artifacts in this book's midriff reflect a select body of student work exhibited during the final pinup. The images and text describe observations of urban spaces defined by politics. They also signal an urgent reminder of the design value site visits and fieldwork hold. They underscore the significance of empirical analysis as an essential part of seeing, learning, and creating.

STUDIO BRIEF:
(IN)FORMAL L.A.—THE SPACE OF POLITICS
Markus Miessen with Kenny Cupers

Brief

The studio will dive into a week-long urban archaeological study to collectively unpack the complexity of urban space—ranging from the super-informal to the highly established. With an energetic focus on Los Angeles, the studio aims to understand these urban conditions through the lens of politics.

> What constitutes spatial politics today?
> What constitutes the political border between urban stakeholders?

Taking into account the varying backgrounds and skill sets of students, we will work together to research, develop, produce, and archive visual and textual arguments toward a spatial register of politics. Methods of generating knowledge will include photography, mapping, journalistic analysis, writing, filing, and other means of isolating those elements of the urban environment that allow us to start to describe the tactics of space.

We will work from a temporary studio setup, which will act as our morning and evening base. We will start with informal group presentations in the morning and will use the daytime for on-site research in and around sites in Los Angeles of your strategic choice. Daily results will be accumulated, analyzed, and developed from late afternoon onward. The studio will be open twenty-four hours a day.

Anticipated Products

We will produce an informal manual that will elaborate on the kinds of spaces that are interesting in terms of our politico spatial categories. The manual will be developed in the form of templates, with which the different groups of students will work and which will later be presented as a pinup.

WEDNESDAY AUGUST 24

09.00	Meet at Studio
09.15	Introductory Talk by Markus Miessen: “Spaces of (in)formal Political Congregation”
10.00	Talk by Kenny Cupers “Spatial Politics 1: Los Angeles Street Vending”
10.45	Individual Questions / Briefing
11.30	Scouting / Fieldwork

THURSDAY AUGUST 25

09.00	Meet at Studio
09.15	Tutorials
12.00	Talk by Markus Miessen “Spaces of Civic Encounter”
13.00	Scouting / Fieldwork

FRIDAY AUGUST 26

09.00	Meet at Studio
09.15	Tutorials
12.00	Talk by Kenny Cupers “Spatial Politics 2: The Youth Camp: On Camps”
13.00	Scouting / Fieldwork

SATURDAY AUGUST 27

09.00	Meet at Studio
09.15	Tutorials
12.00	Talk by Kenny Cupers “Spatial Politics 3: Housing France”
13.00	Scouting / Fieldwork

SUNDAY AUGUST 28

All day	Scouting / Fieldwork

MONDAY AUGUST 29

09.00	Meet at Studio
09.15	Tutorials
12.00	Final Production

TUESDAY AUGUST 30

09.00	Meet at Studio
All Day	Production & Pinup Installation

WEDNESDAY AUGUST 31

09.00	Meet at Studio: Final Preparation
11.00	Informal Pinup Reception
11.15	Group Presentations I
13.00	Lunch
14.30	Group Presentations II
16.00	The Space of Politics—A Panel Discussion on the Current and Future Creation of Urban Space in the Wake of Cultural and Economic Flux
18.00	Lecture by Markus Miessen "The Nightmare of Participation"

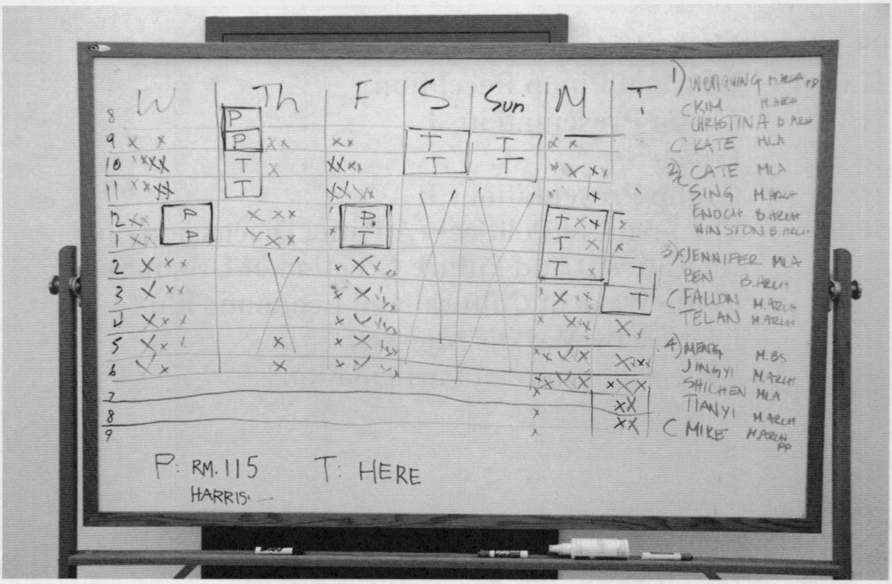

The studio playbook. Photo: Enoch Chow.

Kenny Cupers (left) and Markus Miessen introduce the studio brief.
Photo: Enoch Chow.

Northwest corner of South Broadway and 5th Street, Downtown Los Angeles.
Photo: Yin-Fun Chou.

SOCIOECONOMIC DIVIDES
Yin-Fun Chou

Redevelopment continuously divides socioeconomic activities, marking a visible contrast between modest businesses at the street level and renovated luxury residences above.

Los Angeles Jewelry District
5th St
ONE WAY
ONE WAY
PALACE

Southeast corner of Sunset Boulevard and St. Andrews Place in Hollywood, facing away from the Home Depot, 5600 Sunset Boulevard. Photo: Kathleen Gmyrek.

THE SPACE OF DAY LABORERS

Kathleen Gmyrek

Immigrant workers outside home improvement stores are a familiar sight. Aimed at formalizing the hiring process, "worker centers" have emerged at certain stores to control unsightly, illegitimate, and unauthorized labor practices. However, the formality of these centers, their rules and regulations, detract workers from signing up and shoppers from hiring. Many workers say they are more likely to find work in the informal spaces of the street.

HERMANOS

Iglesia Evangelica Jesucristo, Camino de Verdad, 1830 West Pico Boulevard, Los Angeles. Photo: Kathleen Gmyrek.

CHURCH AND STREET
Kathleen Gmyrek

Latino storefront Pentecostal churches offer a safe and welcoming meeting place where food vendors, sidewalk sales and other transitory activities inside or in front of the church occur. These activities blur the boundaries between private church space and the public sidewalk.

Stopping at the intersection of Vine Street and Hollywood Boulevard.
Photo: Christina Soyoung Hwang.

TERRITORIES OF REPRIEVE
Christina Soyoung Hwang

Reprieve
verb \ri-'prēv\
1. to postpone the punishment of; esp., to postpone the execution of (a person condemned to death)
2. to give temporary relief to, as from trouble or pain

Inside a car, personal territory extends beyond the vehicle. It expands when moving fast and shortens when slowing to a halt — altering one's spatial perception. When an object trespasses this invisible elastic boundary, a feeling of discomfort emerges from the possibility of physical confrontation, pain, or the potential of death.

Two city blocks between Long Beach Avenue and South Alameda Street at East Martin Luther King Boulevard and East 41st Street. Photo: Jennifer Renteria.

(UN)SETTLED TERRAINS 1

Jennifer Renteria

Acquired in 1986 by the City of Los Angeles through eminent domain, this 14-acre site was intended for a waste-to-energy incinerator, until local opposition led to the project's demise. In 1994, the Los Angeles Regional Food Bank was permitted to use the fallow site as a community garden—forming the "South Central Farmers Feeding Families."

A heated legal battle ensued when the previous owner, Ralph Horowitz, fought to repurchase the land. Horowitz won the legal battle in 2003. Once one of the largest urban farms in the country, by 2006, the South Central Farm was bulldozed amids protest and widespread media coverage. Today, the land remains vacant, occupied only by a handful of squatters, including Juan (pitured), who retrofitted parts of an underground drainage system to serve as his home.

Spring Street between 4th and 5th Streets, Downtown Los Angeles.
Photo: Catherine Rilla.

ACCOMMODATION AND DETERRENCE

Catherine Rilla

Living on the street may seem like a solitary existence. However, despite urban policies and design strategies that discourage homelessness on the streets, communities develop, cliques-form, and social networks materialize to create an alternative mapping of public space — shopping carts become mobile storage units and makeshift shelters transform sidewalks into places of refuge.

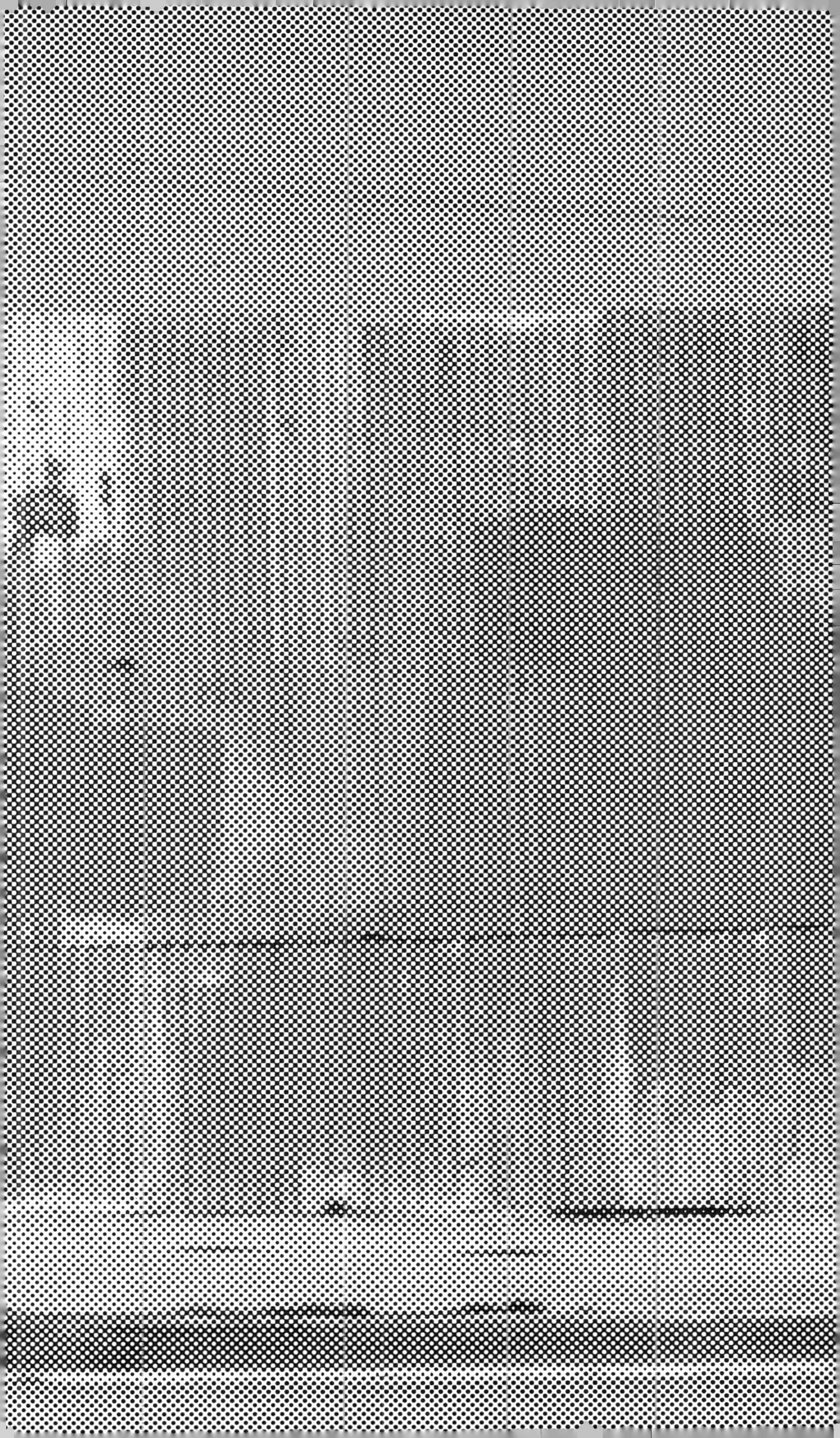

TRASH

Victor J. Jones

Certain works of art and architecture can be considered trash, but when is trash art? Spolia and Arte Povera are two examples at either end of the historical spectrum where refuse is transfigured into art. Constantine's triumphal arch in Rome uses reclaimed sculptural elements from previous buildings. Luciano Fabro composed sculptures from commonplace materials and used wares to create works such as *Pavimento (Tautologia)*. Whether from the spoils of war during Roman antiquity or resistance to modernism and technology in Italy during the 1960s, their practices crafted cultural relevance from discarded matter.

In line with these instances is assemblage art, which has had a hand in shaping art and architecture in Los Angeles for almost a century. This essay travels into Watts, moving past the familiar path of violence in this legendary part of Los Angeles to revisit experiments with trash that began there in the 1920s. The story reveals how today a grassroots nonprofit arts organization, its director, and a handful of architects, artists, and neighborhood residents are working together to refurbish a row of dilapidated houses along East 107th Street. Their collective efforts and participative production weave art and architecture from detritus and the everyday to build and sustain an alternative vision for this underserved community. The trail of unexpected combinations and juxtapositions begins at the end of a narrow street under a monument made of rubbish—the Watts Towers.

While visiting Los Angeles for the first time (to attend the opening of his 1963 *Elvis* exhibition at Ferus Gallery), Andy Warhol bought a sixteen-millimeter sync-sound Bolex camera and shot his partially improvised riff on the Hollywood adventures of Tarzan.[1] In *Tarzan and Jane, Regained, Sort of...*, a free-spirited cast of artists and actors roams the tangled web of freeways and unlikely destinations that replace the wilderness of a jungle. The Beverly Hills Hotel swimming pool substitutes for a lagoon and the Watts Towers stand in for trees,

1 The purchase of the Swiss black box marked the beginning of a five-year period during which Warhol directed and produced over sixty experimental films. For more information about the films of Andy Warhol, consult *Andy Warhol's Blow Job*, by Roy Grundmann, and *The Black Hole of the Camera: The Films of Andy Warhol*, by J.J. Murphy.

vines, and low-lying flora. Midway through the film, Tarzan rests with a dog under one of the smaller structures of the Watts Towers. The narrator whispers, "Jane has been changed into a dog by the forces of evil."

Ominous forces are not alien to Watts. The politics that define and shape the place are murky. Infamously dark tales of corruption, dubious business deals, discriminatory policies, and corrosive public services have transformed the once placid 220-acres of alfalfa fields and livestock farms from a thriving multiethnic, working-class community into one of the earliest examples of a twentieth-century American ghetto.[2] Well before the decay that ravaged most American inner cities during the late 1960s and 1970s, Watts became the embodiment of destructive urban practices.[3] On August 11, 1965, on the one-hundredth anniversary of the Thirteenth Amendment enactment to the United States Constitution, America's most violent social uprising ignited in Watts, only to be followed twenty-eight years later by another. Subsequently, the notorious 1965 Watts Riots and the 1992 Rodney King Riots have cast dark shadows on the region.

Not surprisingly, many Angelinos never venture to this 2.5-square-mile section of southeast Los Angeles. For most, Watts resides in the collective psyche as a euphemism, a one-word cautionary tale of persistent cultural, social, and economic tension. What the novelist Thomas Pynchon wrote in 1966 still rings true: "Watts is country which lies, psychologically, further than most whites seem at present willing to travel.... Yet, in the daytime's brilliance and heat, it is hard to believe there is any mystery to Watts. Everything seems so out in the open, all of it real, no plastic faces,

2 Known as the "crossroads of Los Angeles," Mexican, African, and Asian Americans worked and lived alongside White Americans in Watts from the early 1900s until the late 1950s, when Watts suffered the effects of white flight, due to the early erosion of jobs in heavy manufacturing. In addition to the struggles of urban restructuring, redlining, and freeways, right wing politics pressured Jews and other white ethnics to leave peacefully integrated neighborhoods for white suburbs. Sarah Schrank, "Nuestro Pueblo: The Spatial and Cultural Politics of Los Angeles," in *The Spaces of the Modern City: Imaginaries, Politics, and Everyday Life*, ed. Gyan Prakash (Princeton: Princeton University Press, 2008), 276.

3 Unemployment, decreased home ownership, and the loss of public transportation were provoked by practices such as racial discrimination, restrictive housing covenants, and redlining policies intended to limit where populations could live based on race and ethnicity. Schrank, 276.

no transistors, no hidden Muzak, or Disneyfield landscaping, or smiling little chicks to show you around. Not in Raceriotland. Only a few historic landmarks..."[4]

At the heart of Watts on East 107th Street stands the neighborhood's best-known historic landmark—the Watts Towers (figure 1). Stained by neglect and fierce social uprising, the towers are a memento of the neighborhood's other legacy, assemblage art. Seventeen structures in the form of tall spires, elaborate fountains, and gazebos are nestled in a triangular parcel of land left over from the Pacific Electric Railroad line. Each spindly edifice is hand crafted from bent rebar and caked on cement mortar carefully encrusted with little pieces of broken glass, ceramic tile, and seashells in ornate mosaic patterns. Starting in 1921, Simon Rodia, an Italian immigrant, spent thirty-four years building what he endearingly called *Nuestro Pueblo*. Ultimately, with the neighborhood in rapid decline, the oeuvre and its artist fell prey to ridicule and petty vandalism. Rodia deeded the artistic work and property to a neighbor before leaving definitively in 1954.

Figure 1 Young men hang out at Simon Rodia's Watts Towers, 1966. Photo: Bill Ray © Time & Life Pictures/Getty Images.

Much debate circulated around the towers' fate. Venomous critics condemned their eccentric character as nothing more than heaps of garbage. Among those anxious to see the towers demolished were officials from the Los Angeles Department of Building and Safety who, in 1957, attempted to tear them down. Simultaneously, adventurous artists and actors, architects

4 Thomas Pynchon, "A Journey into the Mind of Watts," *New York Times*, June 12, 1966, 264.

and engineers, historians and journalists, as well as museum directors and international luminaries, converged to preserve one man's expressive assemblage of found objects. Their advocacy not only produced an unprecedented solidarity to save and protect the towers, but also fostered a cultural movement in Watts where art became a tool for social change.[5]

By 1964, the towers had become a contested site for local artistic and cultural activity operating outside of the art world's institutionalized circles. Without access to galleries, museums, and publishing, artists began experimenting with ideas of community building to reimagine their creative role and purpose. The racial tension growing in Watts at the time offered an ideal stage from whence to pronounce an alternative vision to the violent protests. Artists such as Noah Purifoy, Dale Brockman Davis, John Outterbridge, Betye Saar, and Charles Dickson believed political aims could be achieved through aesthetic means.[6] Trash became the predominant medium as objets trouvés and everyday items were reconfigured into expressive works of art. Sharing a commitment to art as a means of social change, Purifoy and Outterbridge became known for their Duchampian interprtations using debris and junk from the 1965 Watts riots.[7] Unfortunately, little historical research has been devoted to this creative renaissance in Watts, which spanned two decades, and its significance to the realm of participatory art practices and cultural production remains underexplored.[8]

In the aftermath of the Rodney King Riots, the Museum of Contemporary Art in Los Angeles presented *UNCOMMON SENSE*. The 1997 exhibition was a timely appraisal of artists

5 Cécile Whiting, *Pop L.A.: Art and the City in the 1960s* (Berkeley: University of California Press, 2006), 138–65.

6 Curtis J. Carter, *Watts: Art and Social Change in Los Angeles, 1965–2002* (Milwaukee, WI: Haggerty Museum of Art, Marquette University, 2003)

7 Noah Purifoy's Joshua Tree Outdoor Museum displays Purifoy's assemblage sculptures, all created on-site between 1989 and 2004, on 7.5 acres of open land. John Outterbridge's *The Rag Factory* (2011) was a site-specific installation commissioned by and exhibited at LA><ART in Los Angeles as part of the Getty initiative Pacific Standard Time.

8 For a more detailed overview of the Watts art movement, consult Curtis J. Carter, *Watts: Art and Social Change in Los Angeles, 1965–2002*; Cécile Whiting, *Pop L.A.: Art and the City in the 1960s*, 138–65; and Kellie Jones, *Now Dig This!: Art and Black Los Angeles, 1960–1980* (Los Angeles: Hammer Museum, 2011).

engaged in public participation and social interaction. One of the six contributing artists, Rick Lowe, created the Watts House Project (WHP), a pilot art initiative addressing the neighborhood immediately surrounding the Watts Towers.[9] Over the course of the installation, neighborhood residents, local artists, business leaders, city officials, and others vocalized their vision for East 107th Street. They concluded the neighborhood should be further developed as an artists' district by reinforcing the existing community arts and education youth centers surrounding the fabled towers. In addition, they resolved that more services should be provided to the influx of art tourists that visit the towers each year. Following the installation, Lowe, with the assistance of Los Angeles-based artist Edgar Arceneaux, continued to organize community efforts and develop a strategic plan for initiating WHP.

In 2007, Arceneaux and Sue Bell Yank, assistant director of academic programs at the Hammer Museum, officially launched Watts House Project. Its founders, eager to reinforce the cultural legacy surrounding the towers, set out to delineate anew how art and architecture could operate as a catalyst for economic and community development. In the spirit of assemblage art practices, WHP enlists neighborhood residents, artists, architects, and scholars to reimagine collaboratively a social, political, and spatial trajectory for process-based projects outside conventional forms of practice. As with earlier Watts art projects, the work emerges organically from the untidy and everyday. The gritty "hands on" approach wrestles with the unpredictable and provisional to broaden the concept of architecture and art and the processes that define each discipline. Artist John Outterbridge, who was director of the Watts Towers

9 Rick Lowe founded Project Row Houses in Houston, where he transformed twenty-two row houses into an art center equipped with artists' housing, a sculpture garden, and an art park. Lowe began meeting with residents in the Northern Third Ward district to imagine how this historic and struggling African American neighborhood could be reimagined in an economically sustainable way. Project Row Houses has evolved from a single block to span six and a half blocks of buildings. It has spearheaded a major artists' residency program and helped boost the community's basic services and infrastructure. Many similar problems plague Watts. The 2010 Census report indicates that half of all families in Watts live in poverty, with an average per capita income of $6,681, compared with the national average of 15% who live below the poverty line and a per capita income of $26,558. In Watts, 64% of the residents do not have a high school diploma; nationally, 15% have not obtained a high school diploma.

Arts Center for more than thirty years, describes WHP as unique: "Up until now, the story of gentrification and architectural philosophy, in Watts, didn't include this."[10]

WHP was awarded a significant grant by the Warhol Foundation in 2009.[11] Three subsequent projects—one realized and two proposed—are part of WHP's effort to define a new generation of cultural activism, where the potency of the work is drawn directly from its ability to venture beyond the studio and into the city. One of these projects, the Cerant | Love House, opts for disposable imagery over constructed matter to propagate a cultural agenda. Another, the Garcia House, reassesses flashbacks of life, time, and diminishing memory to create a patchwork of physical spaces otherwise forgotten. The Platform reformulates the wastelands produced by security fences.

The Cerant | Love House

One of the earliest projects initiated by WHP, the Cerant | Love house is a collaborative effort between the studio artist Alexandra Grant, architects Roberto Sheinberg and Arnold Swanborn, and local residents Louis Cerant and Moneik Johnson. Borne from an installation piece by Grant entitled *A Love That Should Have Lasted*, the initial concept was to erect a large-scale sculptural piece using the word *LOVE* to symbolize unity and affection in a place seen more often as divisive and riddled with conflict. In a photomontage by Grant, the language and text-based artist digitally collages the word *LOVE* with an image of the Cerants' home; the word stands upright like a billboard fixed atop of the bungalow (figure 2). The photomontage was meant to act as a lightning rod to attract attention and resources for the realization of the project, which intermingles narrative, message, and spatial dimension. The project took an unexpected

10 Lynell George, "Watts House Project: Art Meets Architecture Near the Towers," *Los Angeles Times*, November 2, 2008.

11 The Warhol Foundation awarded a grant in the amount of $125,000 to WHP. The primary focus of the foundation's grant-making activity is supporting work that is experimental, under-recognized, or challenging in nature. The program has been both proactive in its approach to the field of cultural philanthropy and responsive to the changing needs of artists. A strong commitment to freedom of artistic expression led the Warhol Foundation to play an active advocacy role for artists during the culture wars of the 1990s and continues to inform its support of organizations that fight censorship, protect artists' rights, and defend their access to evolving technologies in the digital age. Blake Eskin, "Making More Andys Possible," *ARTnews*, vol. 101, no. 5 (May 2002), 48.

Figure 2 Alexandra Grant, *Love House*, 2008. Digital photomontage, 5 × 5 inches.

Figure 3 The Garcia House, Tapestry, Escher GuneWardena, 2010.

but fortuitous detour when the architects announced a series of challenges, including insufficient structural support from the existing roof and numerous zoning restrictions from the Los Angeles building department. As a result, the proposed project was never built, but the photomontage took on a life of its own.[12] An object in its own right, the *LOVE* image is a mechanism of popular culture that takes many forms and connects directly with the hearts and minds of the public, becoming an instrument for fundraising and garnering support for WHP from institutions and individuals.

The Garcia House

The Garcia House compound consists of several structures that accommodate three generations of one tight-knit family. The design scheme of hodge-podge elements, by architects Frank Escher and Ravi GuneWardena, adds necessary living space for the second-generation family members who cohabit the compound and remodeled the bathrooms and kitchens to keep them in functioning order. In addition to addressing these more prosaic needs, the architects, in collaboration with the artists' collective *Slanguage*, developed a distinctive identity for the family's home through a series of interventions. The first is a memory book tracing the family's history in the neighborhood; second is an artwork in the form of a reliquary to enshrine the family book; and third are decorative architectural elements interwoven in the architectural fabric of the home. For example, a new carport, doubling as an outdoor dining pavilion, serves as a communal gathering space for family festivities (figure 3).

The Platform

Security is a preoccupation for all people living on East 107th Street. Fences surround every property, including the Watts Towers, creating an archipelago of safety zones. The ubiquitous infrastructure of fear is a localized notion of border control and defense against urban terrorists. To ease their severity, some of the fences are embellished reflections of Simon Rodia's towers, such as the work of self-taught sculptor Raul Curiel, which is sprinkled throughout the neighborhood. Nonetheless, as Mike Davis points out in *City of Quartz*, "We live in 'fortress cities' brutally divided between 'fortified cells' … Today's colossal scale of residential and commercial security

12 Phone interview with Alexandra Grant, April 20, 2013.

supplants residual hopes for urban reform and social integration..."[13] The Platform is an inverse of the fortress phenomenon. The design compresses a new fence against the fronts of two rundown structures that WHP purchased in 2009 to house their offices and a variety of community amenities. In direct collaboration with WHP's executive director Edgar Arceneaux, managing director Will Sheffe, and program director Trinidad Ruiz, the project set out to strengthen the neighborhood's sorely lacking civic amenities by providing a point of interest that serves the institutional needs of WHP as well as the community. My firm, Fièvre + Jones, designed and built the Platform along with community resident Genaro Alvarez and student volunteers from the University of Southern California School of Architecture.

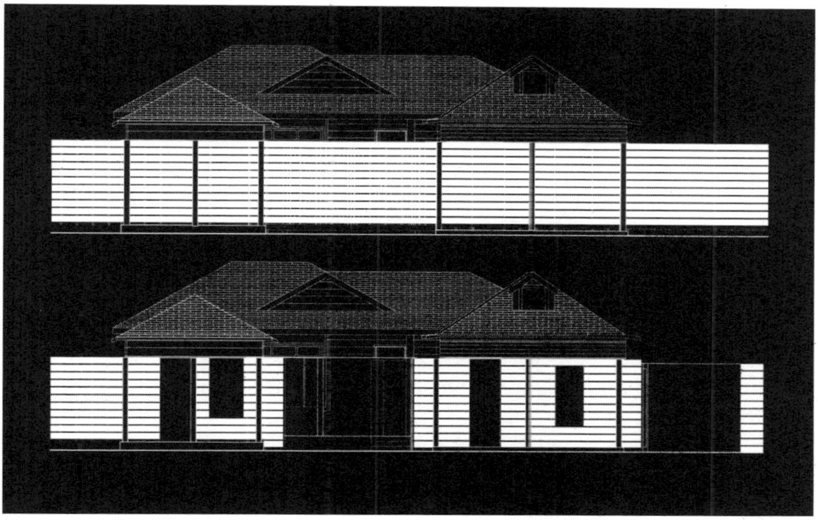

Figure 4 Drawing indicating closed and opened position of the new Watts House Project Platform, Fièvre + Jones, 2010.

The relocation of the property enclosure allows the Platform to respond to a variety of performative needs with minimal resources and complexity. The two houses share a courtyard and are connected by gates that act as a visual marker for the activities within; more importantly, they are unified by a screen of "hardiplank" slats painted in primer white, which do double duty as visual organizers and as security devices (figure 4). Event spaces, such as a coffee shop and intimate yet public spaces that residences and visitors can use at all times, are defined by the simple act of opening and closing the various doors, gates,

13 Mike Davis, *City of Quartz* (New York: Vintage Books, 1990), 224.

and window shutters integrated into the single surface (figures 5 and 6). The ubiquitous bars on doors, windows, and around yards constitute a negative infrastructure in the community, highlighting fear and uncertainty. By transforming this infrastructure into an aesthetic element, rather than foregrounding fear the two houses bespeak unity and modernity.

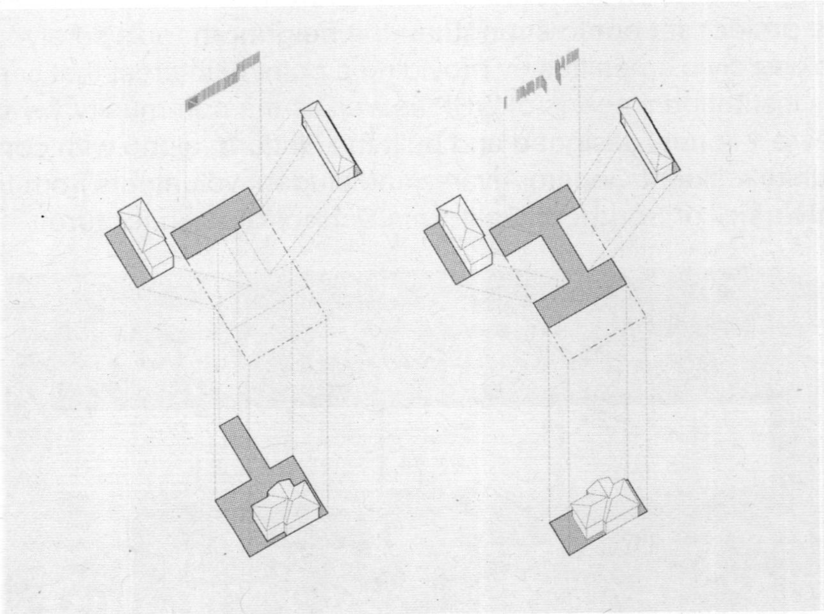

Figure 5 Diagram indicating the spatial variation of the Watts House Project Platform.

Figure 6 The Watts House Project Platform with the Watts Towers in the background, October 2012. Photo: Eric Staudenmaier.

Margins of Opportunity

These three projects in Watts re-conceptualize conventional notions of place, space, and the street in order to capitalize on margins of opportunity that would otherwise go fallow. Questions of where art and architecture overlap are coupled with broader issues of public policy, zoning, and land use. The projects conflate physical and perceptual structures to call out and alter space and offer a positive sense of place in an otherwise daunting political reality.

Instead of evoking destructive behavior or unwarranted circumstances, trash draws connections between seemingly unrelated artists who acknowledge and confront a constellation of physical and cultural differences. Their cultural production challenges a singular vision of creative practice and raises awareness of the *other.* Simon Rodia, Andy Warhol, Noah Purifoy, John Outterbridge, and their contemporaries contributed to a way of seeing and making that demonstrates the ability of art and architecture to be a catalyst as well as disperse forces on behalf of social change—reinforcing art and architecture's necessity in brokering a complex world. The artists and architects working today in Watts and with the Watts House Project carry forward that vision in art, architecture, and infrastructure projects that endow Watts with a proud public face, the beginning of a much longer journey.

SPEEDING
Reid Cigolle

Speeding through the vast desertscapes of the American Southwest, time and space are held by the rhythmic repetition of pumping stations along the Interstate—signals of progress within an otherwise vacant vista. Leaving his hometown of Oklahoma City in 1956, artist Ed Ruscha cataloged this experience as he moved toward Southern California. He later recreated this journey in his 1963 book *Twentysix Gasoline Stations* (figure 1), composed of black-and-white photographs taken between Los Angeles and Oklahoma City.[1] This project, along with his subsequent books, illustrates the artist's indexical approach for making sense of his new city—an alien world that required him to devise original methods of documentation and presentation in order to operate within it. At the beginning of the 1970s, work from Ruscha's books appeared in two seminal publications: Reyner Banham's *Los Angeles: The Architecture of Four Ecologies* and Robert Venturi and Denise Scott Brown's *Learning from Las Vegas*.

Leaving the pedestrian cities of Europe and the Eastern United States for the sprawling cities of the Mojave Desert, Banham and Venturi and Scott Brown set out to understand urban form and function in places affected by increased speed. In stark contrast to works such as Colin Rowe and Fred Koetter's *Collage City*, which relies almost entirely on planometric readings of the relationship between figure and void, these two publications realize the limited value of such an approach when trying to document auto-centric cities. In order to conceive and convey their ideas, each author employs original modes of documentation and conceptualization, based on Ruscha's method.

1 James Ellroy, "Ed Ruscha," *Ed Ruscha: Fifty Years of Painting* (London: Hayward, 2009) 9.

Figure 1 Edward Ruscha, *Every Building on the Sunset Strip* (Los Angeles, 1966).

The Architecture of Persuasion

Learning from Las Vegas sets out to understand and clarify the roles of signage and vernacular architecture in postmodern American cities. The authors state, "Las Vegas is analyzed here only as a phenomenon of architectural communication."[2] For Venturi and Scott Brown, Ruscha's work reflects a shift in urban grammar and syntax—driving cities are literally read through signage, rather than directly experienced.

Central to Venturi and Scott Brown's analysis of Las Vegas is the role of signage in quickly transmitting information across the vast distances of the Strip. They pronounce, "Symbol dominates space. Architecture is not enough. Because the spatial relationships are made by symbols more than by forms, architecture in this landscape becomes symbol in space rather than form in space."[3] Urbanism and architecture are reconfigured to meet increases in velocity and area.

In the chapter entitled *The Architecture of Persuasion,* Venturi and Scott Brown present the changing relationship between signs and space at increasing speeds of perception. For the authors, persuasion operates as a commercial force and is seen in a business' attempt to attract customers. Moving at 3 mph through a bazaar or medieval street, signs may be small since the visual or olfactory qualities of the goods are themselves used to attract customers. However, when speeding past a shopping center at 50 mph, goods cannot be seen until they are ready to be purchased; large signs and symbolic forms must take on the persuasive role of the actual goods.

When navigating the bazaar, moments on the street are registered via perceptive information such as sight and smell. In this way, pedestrians define a place in their mind. The large-scale developments of the Sunset and Las Vegas Strips lack the intricacies of the bazaar, and the automobile makes it nearly

2 Robert Venturi, Denise Scott Brown, and Robert Izenour, *Learning from Las Vegas* (Cambridge, MA: MIT Press, 1972), 5.

3 Venturi, Scott Brown, and Izenour, 13

Figure 2 Mason Williams, Edward Ruscha, and Patrick Blackwell, *Royal Road Test* (New York: Wittenborn, 1967).

impossible to read the subtle differences between individual buildings. When looking at each strip elevation, the sign dominates. Elements are held in order not by the memory of experience, but by indexical devices such as addressing and street names. Signage grows to dominate architecture; the viewer need no longer rely on experience in order to navigate a city.

In 1967, Ruscha and friends Mason Williams and Patrick Blackwell created a 60-page book documenting the destruction of a typewriter. The machine was thrown out of a Buick moving 90 mph along Route 91 in the Mojave Desert. Entitled *Royal Road Test* (figure 2), the piece has the style of detective work and reveals two destructive forces: horizontal speed and vertical impact.[4] The careful documentation here makes clear the force with which the typewriter hit the ground—demonstrated by the shattering of its component parts and the small crater left in the desert dirt. The speed of travel is apparent in the distance between parts of the typewriter—measured by the disarray of parts.

This mapping of parts strewn across land is echoed by Venturi and Scott Brown as they study the latent commercial forces underlying the growth of Las Vegas. The *Comparative Activity Patterns* diagrams (figure 3) found in *Learning from Las Vegas* highlight the locations of repetitive objects. They create an index of churches, groceries, wedding chapels, and automobile renters. This index is further color-coded based on dates-of-establishment. Similar to the typewriter's scattered pieces, the dots of these maps reveal varied commercial and political forces at work. The concentric spread of churches and groceries, with newer establishments found near the edges of the city, explains the residential growth from the center toward the periphery. Elsewhere, the tight clusters of wedding chapels, on the strip or the auto rental sites near the airport make visible the effects of tourism.

4 Mason Williams, Edward Ruscha, and Patrick Blackwell, *Royal Road Test* (New York: Wittenborn, 1967), 3.

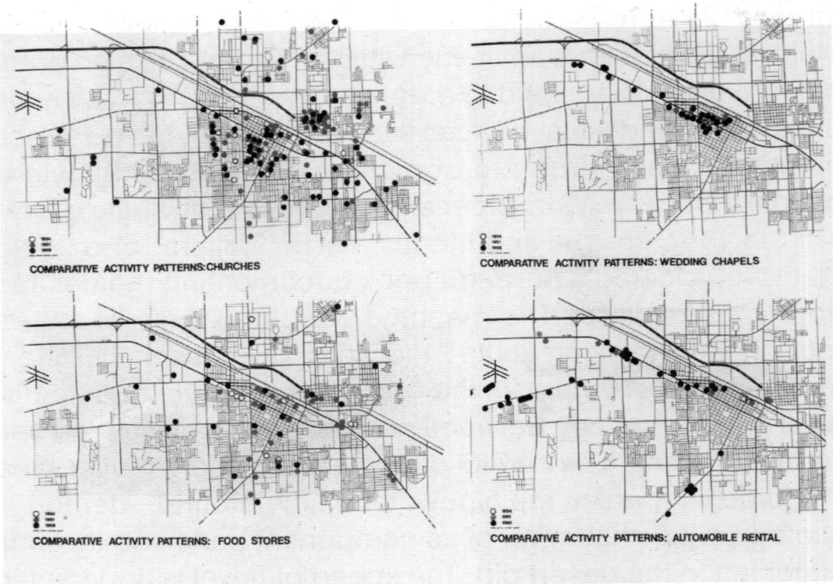

Figure 3 Image from Robert Venturi, Denise Scott Brown, and Robert Izenour, *Learning from Las Vegas: The Forgotten Symbolism of Architectural Form* (Cambridge: MIT Press, 1972).

The Plains of Id

Reyner Banham approaches the work of Ruscha not as someone looking to explain postmodern cities, but as someone trying to understand a specific city. With *Los Angeles: The Architecture of Four Ecologies*, Banham proclaims a desire to "present the architecture (in a fairly conventional sense of the word) within the topographical and historical context of the total artifact that constitutes Greater Los Angeles."[5] Banham's research centers on understanding Los Angeles—a sort of guidebook for the city—focused on explaining its growth and variations.

According to Banham, the most important force in Los Angeles is speed. When considering how to read Los Angeles

5 Reyner Banham, *Los Angeles: The Architecture of Four Ecologies* (Middlesex: Pelican, 1971) 23.

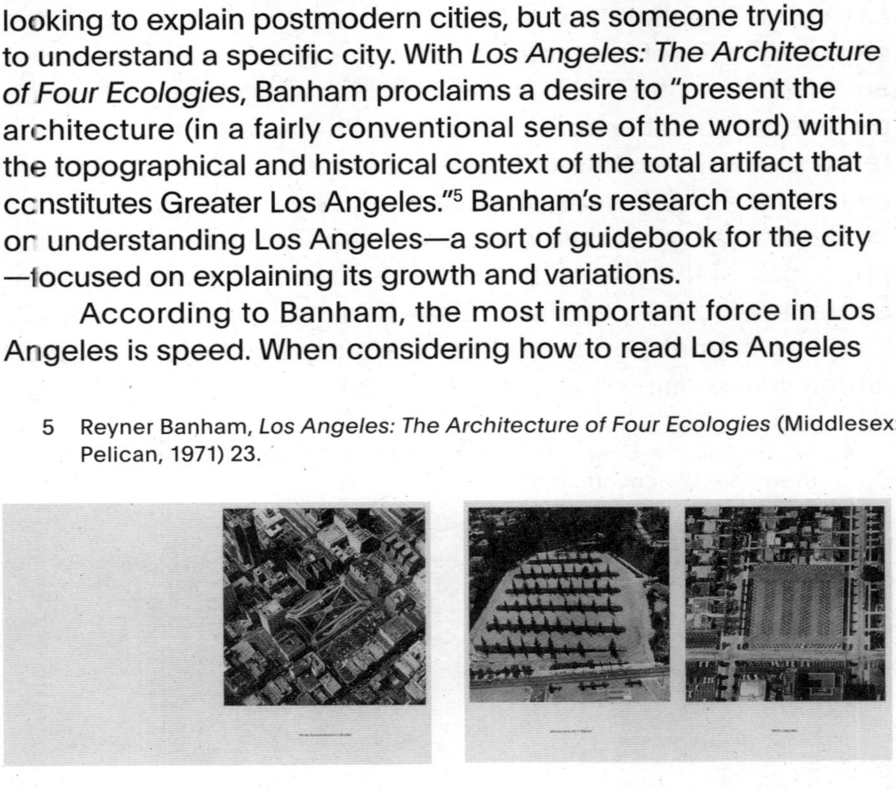

Figure 4 Edward Ruscha, *Thirtyfour Parking Lots in Los Angeles (Los Angeles, 1967).*

(in relation to previous urban examples) Banham writes, "How then to bridge this gap of comparability. One can most properly begin by learning the local language; and the language of design, architecture, and urbanism in Los Angeles is the language of movement."[6]

Ruscha's 1967 book *Thirtyfour Parking Lots in Los Angeles* (figure 4) deals directly with movement by focusing on spaces where cars are idle. Here cars and speed are given weight by casting them in a narrative. This narrative is internal to the city, and told via index. Banham places many of Ruscha's photographs directly into his book; however, they appear as singular instances rather than in Ruscha's repetitive layout. Less interested in the large-scale indexing typical of *Learning from Las Vegas*, Banham studies each parking lot in its own context to make sense of subtle differences. While Ruscha's index allows the city to be read from a car, his style of documentation highlights not just similarity and standard forms, but also difference. It becomes easy to spot small, individual alterations when the primary forms are the same.

Ruscha's aerial photographs, which he hired a helicopter pilot to execute, appear in Banham's book. Banham uses these photographs to explore the specific forces underlying unique qualities at each site. For Banham, the ubiquity of parking lots is the inevitable result of a car-based urbanism; however, it is through the deeper understanding of each lot that he manages to arrive at a unique and informed view of Los Angeles. Banham reinserts the sensibility of the medieval street into Los Angles, slowing down his pace through the city in order to carefully understand spaces that are generally unremarkable and overlooked.

Banham understands Los Angeles through four ecologies: Surfurbia, Foothills, Autopia and the Plains of Id. Significant to this discussion is the Plains of Id—Banham's title for the sprawling basin held between ocean and mountains and filled with

6 Ibid.

a seemingly endless grid of city. Several of Ruscha's books deal directly with these landscapes, but of specific interest to Banham is the role of domesticity therein. Most relevant to Banham's research is Ruscha's *Some Los Angeles Apartments* (figure 5). This book includes many images of dingbat apartments, a predominant housing typology in Los Angeles (favored for its accommodation of covered parking). Taken from the street, Ruscha shows most of the apartments from an oblique view in order to capture the front façade and sides.[7] Banham describes the two sides of the Dingbat's appearance: "The dingbat, left to its own devices, often exhibits the basic characteristics of a primitive modern architecture. Round the back, away from public gaze, they display simple rectangular forms and flush smooth surfaces, skinny steel columns and simple boxed balconies, and extensive overhangs to shelter four or five cars. But out the front, dingbats cannot be left to their own devices; the front is a commercial pitch and a statement about the culture of individualism."[8] Banham's reading prods beyond the simple opinion that the Plains of Id are nothing more than a monotonous, uninteresting service area; instead, he finds within them a subconscious desire for individualism and homesteading.

In a city valuing the single-family house as the supreme symbol of success and personal identity, the dingbat would seem a parasite. However, Banham cleverly understands the role of the dingbat's front façade in keeping up the atmosphere of distinct structures throughout the city, explaining, "The dingbat ... is the true symptom of Los Angeles' urban Id trying to cope with the unprecedented appearance of residential densities too high to be subsumed within the illusions of homestead living."[9] Consequently, he reads the dingbat not as a meaningless

7 Edward Ruscha, *Some Los Angeles Apartments* (Los Angeles: Anderson, Ritchie & Simon, 1965).
8 Banham, 175.

9 Ibid., 177.

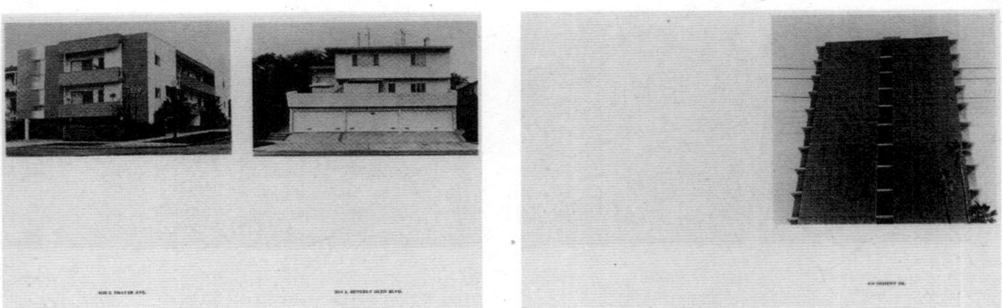

Figure 5 Edward Ruscha, *Some Los Angeles Apartments* (Los Angeles: Anderson, Ritchie & Simon, 1965).

occurrence nor as an unwanted abnormality, but as a necessary compromise between housing needs and civic appearances. Banham grasps the ability of the dingbat to uphold the sense of single-family housing and individual plots of land in a city that treasures these qualities. Read through the eyes of Banham, Ruscha's indices are then not an exercise in expressing the monotony of Los Angeles, but an attempt to glean its subtle differences and complex compromises of aesthetic quality and civic necessity.

Urban Index

Whether highlighting similarity or difference, Ruscha's work is uniquely suited to conceptualizing high-speed cities because it is borne of such places. His monotonous imagery performs the experience of navigating Los Angeles and other similar cities, and is vital in shaping the methodologies of Venturi and Scott Brown and Banham. Fundamentally, the works presented from Los Angeles and Las Vegas are attempts to better understand one's position in space and time. They deal with how we perceive the world around us and, more importantly, how we conceptualize this information. The work should serve as a reminder that we must not only learn how to make cities, but also learn how to better use and understand the ones we already have.

Editor's Notes on Outtakes from the Space of Politics—A Panel Discussion

The Space of Politics—A Panel Discussion was moderated by Victor J. Jones and Warren Techentin. Panelists were Frances Anderton, Orhan Ayyüce, Teddy Cruz, Kenny Cupers, Joseph Giovannini, David Gissen, Qingyun Ma, Stefano de Martino, Markus Miessen, Marcos Sánchez, Roger Sherman, and Rochelle Steiner.

While Reyner Banham's exploratory spirit and curiosity embodied the studio's ethos, The Space of Politics—A Panel Discussion channeled Henri Lefebvre's *Right to the City*.[1] The discussion veered away from purely aesthetic, historical, or technological preoccupations and into debates over the currency of politics in design thinking.

This edited transcript identifies the disparate vantages and camps of a dozen panelists. The cacophony of assertions and reactions is organized according to pertinent themes in an attempt to render the event with greater clarity. Moderator Warren Techentin begins the discussion by introducing the Paris Peace Accords table design to challenge beliefs about space, its production, and its uses. Here Techentin points out that even very small transient elements, like furniture, can become integral parts of a discursive language in space.

A brief dialogue about the unique urban structure of Los Angeles follows. The city's vastness, its atomized nature, and its tenuous urban fabric make Los Angeles a unique example of the influence politics wield over space.

The conversation quickly diverges from the subject of Los Angeles. Debates about design discourse, the academy, and professional practice ensue. Some caution that architecture is changing rapidly—"starchitecture" has run its course—and the need to reevaluate core values is crucial. Others insist that architecture must take on more than aesthetics and formal exploration to be relevant in the 21st century. Panelists vigorously debate the virtues and deficiencies of current practices and pedagogies.

1 Henri Lefebvre, *Le Droit à la Ville*, 1st English edition (London: Wiley-Blackwell, 1992).

OUTTAKES FROM THE SPACE OF POLITICS
A PANEL DISCUSSION
Edited by Stefano de Martino and Victor J. Jones

Los Angeles
Observations on a Post-Industrial City

Warren Techentin Design has an important role in politics. For example, before negotiations between the United States and Vietnam concerning the independence of South Vietnam, a long negotiation occurred about the actual table to be used at the conference. The North favored a circular table where all parties would appear to be equal in importance, while the South Vietnamese argued that only a rectangular table was acceptable because it could show two distinct sides to the conflict. Eventually a compromise was reached in which representatives of the northern and southern governments would sit at a circular table with members representing all other parties sitting in individual square tables around them. Clearly, in establishing relationships between people and ideas, space—whether we are talking about the arrangement of individuals in a room or the distribution of objects in the city—creates a context and provokes responses. Let's begin this conversation by asking Markus and Kenny about their impressions of Los Angeles.

Markus Miessen I am surprised how coherent Los Angeles is, with its ongoing web-like fabric. I thought the city would be made of more distinct zones. One of the things we explored in the workshop was the idea of small pockets and nooks that produce informal spaces with a completely different language of use. This is something Kenny has looked into with his previous research on the politics of street vending in Los Angeles.

Kenny Cupers Los Angeles presents a bizarrely horizontal urbanity. Its striking juxtapositions are nothing like those of cities we are familiar with in Europe, the Northeast United States, or elsewhere.

Qingyun Ma Los Angeles doesn't really follow a European model, nor does it resemble Asian cities either. That is why it is so difficult to discuss urbanism anywhere in the world from the platform of Los Angeles. Los Angeles is a model we have yet to come to terms with.

Warren Techentin If you live in Los Angeles, where people live in enclaves that are either imposed upon them or chosen, there is a lack of friction in space.

Joseph Giovannini Since the introduction of the car, space has been dispersed altogether, and that has atomized the political body. In New York, where space collects people, there is implicitly a negotiated space that is political. In Los Angeles, you're always in a car, you're listening to your radio; space is atomized. We now live in this urbanized dispersed political space.

Orhan Ayyüce Los Angeles is becoming more and more a corporate city. There is hardly any public space. It is all becoming commodified corporate space. You almost have to show your driver's license to get into any space, let alone take a picture of it.

Reflections on Difference Defined by Geography and Culture

Victor Jones Europeans seem to be ideologically committed to working through cultural and social questions when thinking about their own cities, buildings, landscapes, and communities. On the other hand, North Americans are mostly preoccupied with iconography and economy, obsessed with the shape and finish of projects for the purposes of branding and creating product. We seem to be more excited about the making and less concerned about civic values.

Stefano de Martino A basic difference between European and American notions of built space is that Europe has a very long history. It has been used and abused and sub-used over the millennia. It is in a state of total entropy. Most cities in the Unites States on the other hand, have been used once, and then mostly discarded. Cities are just left behind.

Teddy Cruz Europe and the United States have come to be defined by an anti-immigration, anti-welfare, anti-government, and anti-public agenda, which is consolidated in a politics of fear that has implications in the construction of territory and institutions. How many more Wall Street bailouts and foreclosures? How much defunding of public education, infrastructure, and health? How many debt-ceiling debates, fake as they may be, and how many Tea Party zealots will be necessary to prompt our own Spring revolution? Tahrir Square will never happen in the United States because there is not a sense of urgency here. With the Arab Spring, the United States and Europe were suddenly exposed to the socioeconomic inequalities they had produced abroad. The irony is that those people who we claim to be terrorists are giving us the best lesson in Democracy 101.

Orhan Ayyüce With the Arab Spring, we are back to looking at cities, questioning whether architecture is relevant at all. Political issues of individual freedom, inequalities between people, the distribution of income, what is allowed and is not allowed in the city. With the recent events, buildings themselves do not have relevance anymore. The only thing that has significance, architecturally, is how buildings operate urbanistically. Tahrir Square was the demarcation point of something that pulled a set of political ideas and reactions together. Architecture's absence in all these events for me was welcome, an open door for architects and urban designers to recognize other priorities, rather than taking every opportunity as a spatial issue driven purely by formal interests or the aesthetics of space.

Digital Practices, the City, and the Education of an Architect

Victor Jones If the conversational limelight in architecture schools is moving away from digital practices and toward a different dialogue about architecture and the city that concentrates on the complexity of urban space as framed by politics, what role can creative practice play within this arena?

David Gissen The digital aesthetic, the sense that the life of the city is within the object and not in the people of the city, is completely disturbing. It has strong political implications: that the life of the city is gone and the life of the object is ascending. Those of us who are aware of that kind of historical trajectory know that politics in many ways is about the artist or architect making the object dead, right? That's why the grid is so critical to me, and why this animist thing is so frightening.

Kenny Cupers One of the main goals of the weeklong studio we organized was to address students in architecture school. In my personal experience, students suffer from staying inside behind a computer screen. We could learn more from going out there, taking photos, and observing how places work. Becoming an anthropologist offers an opportunity to obtain knowledge that is essential to what we do as designers.

Orhan Ayyüce Recognizing the political implications is where architecture schools should play a larger role. With all of the exciting social and economic changes occurring in the world right now, does it make sense to spend the first year of architecture school cutting up cardboard, putting it together, and looking at it to make sure it looks like sculpture, is pleasing, organized, etc.? The question is, "Should we evolve beyond this production of space, and if so, what kinds of spaces and cities should we be thinking about, perhaps without thinking about the architectural space as an isolated topic?"

Qingyun Ma These two approaches somehow find themselves in opposition and polarization within schools. It is something deeply rooted in the fundamentals of the making and manufacturing of our physical spaces, a process that tends to be apolitical.

Joseph Giovannini There is a suggestion that form and content are in some way permanently separated and antagonistic. I do not know if that is necessarily the case.

Markus Miessen I would not say that by necessity someone who is interested in a particular mode of form-generation should be at the same time apolitical, but this is how it is being taught in many places at the moment.

Teddy Cruz The tragedy is that some schools think that community-based projects or the social itself is passé, like a guy with a ponytail and Birkenstocks. We have to transcend these biases. It does not result in an intelligent debate that can critique and frame discussions, pedagogies, or processes of creative practice. By distancing oneself from the sociopolitical and economic realities, the urban propositions of seemingly avant-garde architects become problematic.

Frances Anderton The education of an architect has to go beyond architects teaching architects about architecture. It has to bring in people who engage communities in different ways.

Markus Miessen The non-physical components of design are something that should also be taught in architecture schools. Kenny talked in terms of research and practice. Research needs to be taught, not as something that promotes a dichotomy between research and practice, but rather one that fuses research as part of practice. There shouldn't be architects who reflect and think, while others do and make.

Marcos Sánchez Markus introduced an idea during the workshop that had to do with a curious and interesting use of agonism rather than always negotiating consensus. Why not have blocks within the school of architecture more than simply distinguish computation from urban preoccupations. Why not multiply those fractures to propagate a field of agonism?

Agonism Versus Consensus
Contemplations on Emergent Forms of Practice

Victor Jones What does agonism mean in terms of finding a research project in architecture and urbanism?

Teddy Cruz Embedded in the meaning of agonism is a set of operational practices that are alternative, the opposite of antagonism. I am trying to figure out where we are going with the discussion of digital versus social practices; we seem to be locked into this sort of no-way-out type of antagonism. Agonism I think suggests a very different way of dealing with difference. Chantal Mouffe suggests that agonism is a process by which the political and economic hegemonic project, institutional power, is exposed. The institutional mechanisms are visualized and become the material of the artist. For me, if I want to advance the discussion of affordable housing, it cannot happen without advancing the discussion about the need to transform the politics and economics of housing. I need to understand what produced the crisis in the first place. The exposure and the visualization of conflict becomes a tool, an artistic tool.

Markus Miessen I definitely advocate agonism, and not consensus, between the two factions. I think there should be productive conflict between the two. How should architectural practice be defined and what are the role models for that practice? In conventional terms, the client is quite often important and the architect is underrated, from the point of view of market economy. There is one predominant model that we follow. But there are also questions, especially for students here who are going to become architects in a couple of years. Are you going to be waiting for clients to come to you in a time when clients' demands are on the decline? Or are you going to set up an alternative model of practice?

New Language for Practice
Reassessments of Communication in Design Disciplines

Warren Techentin If "politics" by definition is a process by which groups of people make collective decisions, the word "politics" also has an unsavory character. For some, politics is not seen as a means to collective decision making, but instead a process of persuasion and coercion, co-opted by various personalities and forces of advocacy to narrow ends—often with people who have a financial stake in the decision. How does design deal with this?

Rochelle Steiner The challenge facing architects is not unlike the challenge facing artists who think about how to mobilize their practices in times when they have become so dependent on a market economy and political structure.

Teddy Cruz We need to dive right away into the current urgency, the very strong and possible rethinking of institutions and the roles creative practice plays in engaging the very construction of the political.

Frances Anderton After many years of dealing with communication about conflict, architects and designers are not considered part of the dialogue. It is not that they are not relevant; they are not thought about as participants in the dialogue. When we are talking about the space of politics, I think architects and designers of space have to learn to be politicians. Architects, artists, and designers have to learn to speak a language in order to communicate that they are able to negotiate beyond the solipsistic world of architecture.

David Gissen This idea of consensus is critical to the way we talk about the word "design." The way we think about the idea of design and architecture from a historical perspective has consensus built into it. The term "design" in various European languages and in the English language from the 1920s to, lets say, the 1950s, implied a union between proletariat, bourgeois governance, and industry. The design object itself represents aunion between those three partners. Those three sectors do not exist in the forms they did eighty or ninety years ago. They are completely dispersed: governance is everywhere and nowhere; the social classes—I don't know if I believe in that idea so much—are everywhere and nowhere; and production is everywhere and nowhere. So, we no longer have the language to describe what kind of consensus we would insert ourselves into or what the architectural object would represent. We need to build a new language to describe a new practice that begins to bring together groups that do not have names or forms yet.

Teddy Cruz We have distanced ourselves from the public with our self-referential language. Nevertheless, the language we use should not lessen the complexity of the way we speak, but rather engage the procedures of others. Architects need to know how a developer's pro forma is built, what tax credits are made of, what types of pedagogical tools can allow us to interface with communities and the public, what type of tools we can use to rethink the political itself. So language is the very condition of a crisis that we are trying to get at here. Those protocols are material for design. Rather than being designers of artifacts and buildings, we can also be designers of politics, policies, and economics. The pro forma of the developer becomes the site of the intervention. The pro forma is an instrument to construct community by designing a more intelligent and just relationship across profit margins, sources of income, and resources, and by the designing and reorganization of resources, that is, the material for design. In tandem, a very interesting exploration of formal configurations can hopefully be transparent in those socioeconomic relations as well.

A Social Agenda for Space
Interrogations of Spatial Performance

Victor Jones What are alternative means other than buildings that an architect possesses to create and activate space?

Rachel Berney Are we not talking about a new iconography for people to gather, to do everyday life things, coming almost in pilgrimage? It is the design of our public spaces that points to where the public sphere touches down in physical space. We need to talk about different ways to think about iconography and the spectacle of the everyday, especially since we are moving from big events and big buildings to processes, politics, and interactions at smaller scales.

Markus Miessen Is it not a two-fold question? On the one hand what you referred to as the representative part of architecture does manage to draw more audiences. We want conflict to occur in situations like here, right now, for example. Architects are really good at producing amazing buildings, but most of them are still self-referential gestures at the end.

Joseph Giovannini I think immediately of the City of Music in Rome where Renzo Piano purposely created public spaces in which people gather, or where people can express themselves collectively. When criticizing architects for what is deemed to be hyper-formalism, one has to be more specific about who it is they are talking about. One cannot simply make generalizations about all architects.

Roger Sherman You cannot design conflict. I do not even think it is entirely possible to design for conflict. But what you can do is to look at iconography in a slightly more complex way that is, as you say, not an expression of the architect's own imprimatur, but rather the recognition of embedded identities—a complex object that is recognized by different people as different things. It does not shy away from the semiotic.

Teddy Cruz But we can design conflict and we can design the political! We can design social relations, and this is what has been absent from the debate. There is a dichotomy, and there is a huge rupture at this moment. What unites us in the creative fields is simply our powerlessness to face the current conditions of socioeconomic emergency. There is a world that is falling apart out there, and we need to rethink our relationship with institutions in that context. I am interested in constructing discourse around other issues to obtain crucial detours in the discipline that might not result in building. I believe the future of urbanization will not be led by buildings, but rather by a fundamental reorganization of socioeconomic relations that are occurring now. Architects have a role in designing those relationships. Who is managing those long-term relationships or who has access to these interests in the environment? The issues of management, of long-term community building—all of those are aspects of design that we can engage in tandem with experimental formal practices.

David Gissen The issue, then, is not a spatial one. One of the things that the politics of architecture and urbanism increasingly engages is the politics of environment—the idea that, in addition to providing frameworks for us to express ourselves, cities provide frameworks for us to live in. For me, the issue is an idea of environment that is not sentimental, not naturalistic, in which architects might find a space, some kind of framework that supports life at some very basic fundamental level.

Frances Anderton I got into radio almost twenty years ago following the Los Angeles Riots, when a show called *Which Way,*

L.A.? started. *Which Way, L.A.?* is a very interesting discussion program whose roots lay in the question of what made the riots of 1992 happen. At no point in the public dialogue taking place at the time did one hear very much from architects and designers, although within the architecture and design world there was a part of that event that was galvanizing, architects and designers who absolutely wanted to be part of the solution. They saw the problem as a spatial one, they saw the problems lying in mini-malls, and they saw the problems lying in the inequity of space and environment in some parts of Los Angeles versus other parts of Los Angeles. But in terms of the actual dialogue that took place in the mainstream media, designers and architects did not get much attention.

Markus Miessen Ninety-nine percent of architectural work, from my point of view, does not have an agenda that goes beyond an idea of construction. What we should acknowledge here is that in this space where we are sitting right now, we are talking about architects who maybe make 0.5 percent of spatial production.

Stefano de Martino Architecture and the work most architects do, whether they are big names or not, are probably the last in a long chain of decision makers—politicians, speculators, developers, etc.; architects come at the end of a long process and they have got very little to say, but what they do is definitely political and totally divisive. The moment you draw a line, you generate a here and a there. Even if that line is just a curb or a dividing line in the middle of the road, or a concrete wall dividing one territory from another, it is the most basic act of division. If you address the question of space with architects, of course they will think about cubic meters and making places. But there is another type of space that is simply the relation between different things. That is where the expression David used—"environment"—is probably far closer to an understanding of space as something that is a relationship of many different complex things.

Teddy Cruz We need to seek new sites of intervention and research, new practices, and new procedures that are not embedded with star architects. While the creative intelligentsia of this country and of the world flocked to Dubai and China in the last years of a strong economy to catapult those new centers of power, the best projects being articulated, the ones addressing the political and the social, were happening somewhere else.

They were happening in Latin America, in Medellín, in Bogotá. They were happening in Brazil, where enlightened individuals decided to run for the office of mayor to construct a different conception of the political, to rethink marginal taxation, to rethink the interface with the public, to think that new models of urbanization could emerge by tapping into the potential of social networks and informal economies. Those are the projects we should be looking at, to understand the processes behind them and begin to trace a very different attitude of practice and interface.

AGENCY AND POLITICS IN ARCHITECTURE

Warren Techentin

Los Angeles is famous for its Hollywood agents. An army of these individuals acts on behalf of and represents the skills and expertise of what is known as "the talent." While agents work tirelessly for their clients, they operate in the background —in the metaphorical "back room." They are neither activists nor openly political—nor can they be. Agents work at the behest of others representing the creative talent of both individuals and large studios while orchestrating the assembly of creative teams who are then charged to work together. They hold powerful sway in negotiations between parties—shaping the process significantly without controlling it. In Los Angeles, many agents have themselves become celebrities.

Similar in many ways to their Hollywood counterparts, architects for centuries have acted as agents for their clients' projects and have enjoyed and benefited from this cozy relationship (sometimes also becoming celebrities). Architects organize, design, and implement the work necessary to assure the realization of projects for which they are hired, often assembling and managing large teams of experts and specialists in the service of their clients. Architects navigate the traps and pitfalls of the process—feasibility, permitting, advocacy, and construction. Nearly always the project is someone else's and often at the service of another's political, social, or economic ambitions. Idealism and idiosyncrasy are often tempered or bargained away in the face of the many bureaucratic, life-safety, or political requirements necessary to achieve project completion. Agency, by nature, implies a predetermined need or even willingness towards negotiated consensus, and therefore limits the capacity for activism in a project. The architect's role necessitates a moderating force aimed at project fulfillment. Historically, architects have lacked the capacity to force issues within the political process directly without someone, client or otherwise, imparting agency upon them and underwriting the fees for their services.

The meaning of the word agency itself has expanded in architecture as of late. Parametric modeling software has come to dominate the upper end of architectural production. These modeling systems cast building information into hierarchical relationships with one another through the use of "objects"—sometimes also referred to as "agents." Each "agent" in a parametric model is set in a rigidly fixed—though variable—relationship with other agents, allowing for flexibility and change to be easily propagated amongst the higher or lower orders of the system and ultimately leading to nested sets of predictable relationships between them. These supra-organizational agent-based systems represent the extent to which logistics and project delivery have come to dominate architecture. While this software may be critical for organizing increasingly complex construction projects, parametric systems are worrisome because they indicate the further transformation of architecture into what sociologist Anthony Giddens identifies as an "expert system" or "abstract system" whereby traditional and actual authority is replaced by agency within a field of assumed expertise—thereby limiting the role of the architect to nothing more than a manager of a priori relationships in the process.[1] Designers who fear these synthetic and quantifiable hierarchies have turned to "emergent" or "generative" processes that script (as in Hollywood) agent-based algorithms or behaviors, a bottom-up strategy allowing agent "spontaneity" to impart a touch of humanity in the process. Generative design seeks to fundamentally impact the overall network of relations by incorporating opportunities often omitted from the design process.

Unlike their Hollywood agent counterparts, architects are charged with the crucial task of creating and implementing a project's vision—they design buildings and environments with identity and atmosphere, developing a set of forms, experiences, and relationships. This affords the designer a certain level of power in determining what and how the various forces of any project are to be reconciled and incorporated. Hence, the position of the architect is perpetually caught in-between: contractually operating in the interests of someone else at the same time as being an artist in the critical position of purveying a cultural milieu. Simultaneously agent and talent, service provider and cultural attaché, moderator and visionary—this seemingly schizophrenic duality between the goals of autonomous artistic production and the necessities of project deliver underscores the problematic position of the architect when it comes to political activism. Because of these internal disciplinary

1 Anthony Giddens, "Living in a Post-Traditional Society," in Ulrich Beck, Anthony Giddens, and Scott Lash, *Reflexive Modernization, Politics, Tradition and Aesthetics in the Modern Social Order* (Cambridge: Polity Press, 1994).

conflicts, architecture has avoided the political, or at least has an underdeveloped capacity to deal with its complexities. Perhaps given comfort with their role of defining the aesthetic aspects of their projects, traditionally most architects have abdicated the potential for activism and with it the possibility to shape a truly political project.

Pier Vittorio Aureli argues that architecture—because it makes and forms space—is by nature intrinsically political, allowing each architect and each project the capacity for a kind of activism and political engagement with the city. For Aureli the political act emerges and resides in the material and spatial dimensions of architecture and its response to its expanded environment. The term "project" for him—in lieu of the word "building"—is crucial to differentiate because the word presupposes a theoretical and conceptual foundation that enables the politicization of a project—built or otherwise—beyond mere building. Most importantly, unlike mere buildings, projects have the capacity to propose alternatives to the city that challenge given orders or explore the ideas architects are not being hired to do.

Aureli establishes a fundamental split between urbanism and architecture. For him, architecture is what articulates the political and therefore each project establishes a political position vis-à-vis the city. And if each project is a political position (whether the architect takes one or not), the city then becomes the result of the agonistic struggle between architectures played out over time. Indeed, Aureli's argument lies in reserving the disciplinary space for architecture to speak on its own terms—as the classical "voice" of architecture has traditionally been established through its material substance. Yet, by bracketing off the urban condition as oppositional to and separate from architecture—as almost a neutral field or a "sea of flows" in which life ephemerally floats by—alternative notions of the political are locked out of the process, missing the opportunity to engage the wider landscape of spatial practices that do not always presume to have purely architectural concerns.

> The concept of the archipelago describes a condition where parts are separated yet united by the common ground of their juxtaposition. In contrast to the integrative apparatus of the urbanization, the archipelago envisions the city as the agonistic struggle of parts whose forms are finite and yet, by virtue of their finiteness,

are in constant relationship both with each other and with the "sea" that frames them.[2]

Once we address issues of the urban, it changes the disciplinary limits of architecture beyond isolated conversations about objects and forms. For many years now disciplinary boundaries have been shifting and changing as the urban environment necessitates experts of all sorts. Architecture is one of many spatial practices today to question for our environment and how we produce the so-called parts of the city. The explosion of consultants alongside new media, digital processes, and a demographic majority of the world now residing in a globalized, urban population allows for a critical realignment of how the architect engages urbanism and urban systems. While architecture may be typecast by the objects it presents, the role of the architect is not. As the traditional lead professional for spatial practice, and given the scope of projects today, what if the role of the architect expands to the point that building design becomes just one part of a much larger agenda for what a project is? Project vision still lies firmly in the grasp of the architect, but is managed through consultants specializing in surface effects, algorithms, concrete construction, sustainability, brand management, etc.

Moreover, what if architects—enabled by new participatory communication technologies and open source methodologies—were to suspend the traditional architect-client relationship of agency and instead become leaders in the process of establishing the goals, image, and frameworks under which we build? Markus Miessen alludes to this question in his critique of narrow architectural disciplinarity. He supports a form of agonistic activism that ultimately endeavors to destabilize the comfortable, passive, and doctrinaire position of the agent architect as both service provider and professional building maker[3] in order to engage and even advocate directly for the many unconsidered voices, positions, and forces currently marginalized from architecture and our environments. Meissen asks that we publicly interrogate design and the system of building, which has become burdened under bureaucratic weight, to support a more emergent and generative public life and to "script" alternatives and

2 Pier Vittorio Aureli, *The Possibility of an Absolute Architecture* (Cambridge, MA: MIT Press, 2011), xi.

3 Markus Miessen and Shumon Basar, eds., *Did Someone Say Participate?* (Cambridge, MA: MIT Press, 2006), 23.

challenge assumptions of what an architect does and what architecture can do. Agency in architecture suggests that we trust in new modalities of self-organization and people who share a desire to build in order to nurture an emergent political process about what a project or even our city could be (or should not be)—to establish a super communicative process where all people with a stake in a project—perceived or actual—meet, debate project parameters, seek financing, etc.

As Miessen recognizes, the results will be unpredictable and potentially terminal as we move outside of the rigid categories erected to ensure forms of consensus, in order to achieve new and unprecedented goals for our cities. Perhaps architects, emboldened by new technologies and the capacity to assemble highly specialized, even politicized, teams for each project, will become more like their Hollywood counterparts —inextricably intertwined in the network of communication and relationships for projects and processes they lead, but no longer needing to be in control. I hope architects are able to avoid the fate of the mythical Tower of Babel. Unless architects expand beyond their constrained notion of practice, the very need for the project itself may be ultimately lost.

BIOGRAPHIES

FRANCES ANDERTON is a cultural critic and writer. Her distinctive voice permanently altered the Los Angeles airwaves when she became radio host of KCRW's *DnA: Design and Architecture* in 2002. Frances is also the producer of Warren Olney's daily current affairs shows, *To the Point* and *Which Way, L.A.?,* broadcasted on KCRW and kcrw.com. She is a frequent speaker and writer on West Coast design and architecture, and recently published *Grand Illusion: A Story of Ambition, and Its limits, at L.A.'s Bunker Hill* (2012), a book about Frank Gehry's Research Studio, at the University of Southern California, School of Architecture.

ORHAN AYYÜCE is an architect and writer teaching at California Polytechnic State University, Pomona, Woodbury University, and East Los Angeles College. He is senior editor for *Archinect,* where he has written feature articles about architecture, urbanism, people, politics, arts and culture. Ayyüce's blog *else place* features many spontaneous and conceptual ideas, reviews, images and commentary about the built environment. He serves on the board of directors for Society for Moving Images about the Built Environment, MIBE. He is a member of the editorial board at Architects for Peace and a columnist for *Arkitera* in Istanbul, Turkey. Ayyüce was born in Izmir, Turkey. He lives and works in Los Angeles.

ADAM BANDLER is a designer and curator in New York City. He is the assistant curator for the Arthur Ross Architecture Gallery at Columbia University, where he also teaches in the Critical, Curatorial, and Conceptual Practices in Architecture Program.

RACHEL BERNEY, PHD, is assistant professor in the School of Architecture at the University of Southern. Dr. Berney teaches in the fields of landscape architecture and urban design and planning. She has worked with groups that support community and public space development, including Urban Ecology in the San Francisco Bay area and the Verde Coalition in Los Angeles. Her work has been exhibited in many municipalities and at the Oakland Museum of California. Dr. Berney's research interests include history and theory of urban design and planning with an emphasis on social and environmental factors. Her current research is focused on the use and politics of public space in city remaking projects. Her work can be found in the *Journal of Planning Theory, Journal of Urban Design,* and in the forthcoming edited book *Right to the City in the Global South: Transnational Urban Governance and Socio-Spatial Transformations.*

REID CIGOLLE is a designer, writer and photographer. He received his Master of Architecture from the Yale School of Architecture, where he studied the synthesis of art, architecture and urbanism under Prof. Stanislaus von Moos. Prior to attending Yale, he graduated from the University of Southern California School of Architecture, where he was awarded the AIA Gold Medal as well as the George H. Mayr Traveling Fellowship to execute "on-the-ground" research in the five largest cities of South America. He lives and works in Los Angeles.

TEDDY CRUZ is a professor in Public Culture and Urbanism in the Visual Arts Department at University of California, San Diego, where he founded CUE / Center for Urban Ecologies. He has been recognized internationally for his urban research on the Tijuana-San Diego border, advancing new models of civic participation, affordable housing and public infrastructure at the scale of neighborhoods. He received the prestigious Rome Prize in Architecture, was the first recipient of the James Stirling Memorial Lecture On The City Prize and the Ford Foundation selected him recently for the "Visionary Leader Award," an important recognition given to a few individuals worldwide for their innovative efforts on the front lines of key social issues. His work has been published in the *New York Times, Domus,* and *Harvard Design Magazine.* Most recently, he represented the United States in the Venice Architecture Biennial and his work was included in *Small Scale, Big Change* exhibition at the Museum of Modern Art in New York.

KENNY CUPERS is assistant professor at the School of Architecture, University of Illinois at Urbana-Champaign, where he teaches architectural history and theory. His work focuses on the social agency of architecture and the uses of urban space. Forthcoming books include a history of French mass housing and new town development, an edited volume that examines the problematics of use in architecture and urbanism, and a photographic reportage of the Paris suburbs. His research on the history of modern urbanism, participation, and contemporary urban issues, such as the politics of street vending in Los Angeles, has been published in Positions, *Planning Perspectives, Cultural Geographies, the International Journal of Urban and Regional Research,* and *Thresholds*. Kenny was the 2010–2011 Reyner Banham Fellow at the University at Buffalo and is co-author of *Spaces of Uncertainty* (2002, with M. Miessen), an investigation into the ephemeral qualities of public space through the lens of post-wall Berlin.

DIANE GHIRARDO is professor of the history and theory of architecture at the University of Southern California School of Architecture, where she teaches and researches 20th century architecture, Renaissance architecture, and women's spaces in Renaissance Ferrara and 20th century Italian architecture. Ghirardo's books include *Building New Communities: New Deal America and Fascist Italy* (1989); *Out of Site: A Social Criticism of Architecture* (1992); *Architecture After Modernism* (1996); and *Aldo Rossi: Drawings* (with Germano Celant, 2008). Her forthcoming book, *Italy. Modern Architectures in History* (2013) is from Reaktion Press (London). She has published widely in leading academic journals, including *The Art Bulletin, The Journal of the Society of Architectural Historians, Journal of Architectural Education, Renaissance Quarterly, Oppositions, Telos,* and *Journal of Urban History*. Ghirardo received her PhD in History and Humanities from Stanford University in 1983. She has been a visiting professor at the University of Sydney, Australia; the University of Cape Town, South Africa; Massachusetts Institute of Technology; Rice University, Houston, Texas; and Politecnico of Turin, Italy.

JOSEPH GIOVANNINI is an architect and writer. He has written just about everywhere including the *New York Times, Los Angeles Times, New Yorker, Architectural Record, Domus,* and *Interior Design*. He is currently finishing a history of contemporary architecture. As a critic, he has won awards, grants and honors, from the Art World Magazine/Manufacturer's Hanover Trust for distinguished newspaper architectural criticism, the National Endowment for the Arts, the Graham Foundation, the Los Angeles Chapter of the AIA, and the California Council of the AIA. He has taught advanced and graduate design studios at Columbia University, the University of California, Los Angeles, the University of Southern California, and the University of Innsbruck.

DAVID GISSEN is an historian and theorist of architecture and urbanism, and currently holds the position of associate professor of architecture and visual studies at the California College of the Arts. His recent work concentrates on developing a novel concept of nature in architectural thought and the parameters for an experimental form of practice in architectural history. David is the author of *Subnature: Architecture's Other Environments* (Princeton Architectural Press, 2009), editor of the "Territory" issue of *AD Journal* (2010), and editor of the book *Big and Green* (Princeton Architectural Press, 2003). David lectures on his work internationally with recent invited talks at the University of Southern California, Harvard University, Yale University, Princeton University, The Royal Danish Academy of Art, The Bartlett School of Architecture, and Postopolis! Los Angeles, sponsored by the Storefront for Art and Architecture.

VICTOR J. JONES is an assistant professor of architecture at the University of Southern California, a principal of Los Angeles-based Fièvre + Jones, cultural activist, and writer. His research lies at the intersection of architecture, infrastructure and community building within cities. Recent design projects include the Platform for Watts House Project (2011) and a skate park for New Orleans' City Park (2009). His design work has been supported by numerous grants, including the Graham Foundation, Artplaces, and the Nathan Cummings Foundation. Forthcoming books include *The Basento Aqueduct: Another Side of Infrastructure* (2014). Jones has been published in *AMC/le Moniteur*, the *New Orleans Times Picayune*, *ARTVOICES* and the *Journal of Architectural Education*. Until 2009, he was an assistant professor of architecture at Tulane University. He lives with his partner in Silver Lake.

QINGYUN MA is the dean of the University of Southern California School of Architecture and founder of Shanghai-based architecture firm MADA s.p.a.m. Named one of the world's most influential designers by *Business Week*, Ma's experience and involvement on an international level make him a leader in the design community with a great understanding of the contemporary issues of global urbanization. In 2007, Ma launched the global initiative the USC American Academy in China, a base for visiting scholars to facilitate their research and foster academic exchange. Ma was the chief curator of the 2007 Shenzhen Hong Kong Biennale, and he is frequently invited as a speaker and juror, including for the prestigious Rome Prize and the 2010 Shanghai World Expo. MADA s.p.a.m. has designed and built modern buildings and urban communities, garnering worldwide recognition.

STEFANO DE MARTINO is a professor at the University of Innsbruck, Austria, and co-founder of Lorma Marti, the Berlin-based collaborative he started with Karen Lohrmann in 2002, which focuses on studies of spaces, cultural manifestations, and resultant landscapes. His work engages the shifting tension between a physical and a critical perception of space through different media. He is an editor and author of the periodical *Correspondents; Update: All Possible Worlds* (2008), *how we spent it* (2009), and the forthcoming *WORKBOOK* with Lars Neckel. He taught at the Architectural Association, Columbia University, University of Pennsylvania, the Royal Danish Art Academy, the Berlage Institute and, most recently, the University of Southern California. In 2010 he initiated Urban States, a think-tank on current agendas in the urban domain.

MARKUS MIESSEN is a professor of critical spatial practice at the Städelschule in Frankfurt. An architect and writer, his work revolves around the question of critical spatial practice, institution building, and spatial politics. In various collaborations, Miessen has published: *Actors, Agents and Attendants* (Sternberg Press/ SKOR, 2011), *Waking Up From The Nightmare of Participation* (Expodium, 2011), *The Nightmare of Participation* (Sternberg Press, 2010), *Institution Building* (Sternberg Press, 2009), East Coast Europe (Sternberg Press, 2008), *The Violence of Participation* (Sternberg Press, 2007), and *Did Someone Say Participate? An Atlas of Spatial Practice* (MIT Press, 2006, with S. Basar). Architectural projects include LU Arts Centre (UK), Performa Hubs 09/11 (US), the reappropriation of a former post-office for Manifesta 8 (Spain), and his largest project to date: a masterplan and Kunsthalle building for a former NATO nuclear-warhead bunker facility in Germany. As a consultant, Miessen has advised The European Kunsthalle (Cologne), SKOR (Amsterdam), WIRE (Zurich), and The Government of Slovenia (New York). In 2008, he founded the Winter School Middle East (Dubai & Kuwait). Academic positions include Architectural Association, London (2004–08), Berlage Institute, Rotterdam (2009–10) Hochschule für Gestaltung, Karlsruhe (2010–11), and HEAD Geneva (2011–13).

MARCOS SÁNCHEZ teaches graduate, post-professional, and undergraduate studios as well as seminars in history and theory at the University of Southern California, School of Architecture. He is also a member of the cultural studies and studio faculty at the Southern California Institute of Architecture (SCI-Arc). With Mark Wasiuta, Sánchez is a partner in the office International House of Architecture (IHA). In recent years IHA has developed several projects that examine visual and chemical aspects of Los Angeles's atmosphere. Inversion Layer, initiated during a residency at the Banff New Media Institute, examines smog as a culturally produced object. Instructions for the Reconstruction of Historical Smog was developed from research at the Los Angeles Air Quality Management District and University of California Riverside's Center for Environmental Research and Technology. Sánchez is now working on Air Sampler, an anthology that assembles projects, texts, and topics on the nascent field of air urbanism.

ROGER SHERMAN is principal of Roger Sherman Architecture and Urban Design in Los Angeles and co-director of cityLAB, an urban think-tank at UCLA, where he is also adjunct professor. His work has been featured on CNN, in *Newsweek, Fast Company* and *Metropolis* as well as in numerous books, including *The Infrastructural City* and *On Farming*, both from Actar. His Duck-and-Cover and Playa Rosa projects were exhibited at the 2009 International Architecture Biennale in Rotterdam and the 2010 Venice Biennale, respectively. He is author of several books, including *L.A. Under the Influence: The Hidden Logic of Urban Property* (Univ. of Minn., 2010) *Re: American Dream: New Housing Prototypes for Los Angeles* (Princeton Architectural Press). He is co-editor, with Dana Cuff, of *Fast Forward: After the Master Plan* (Princeton Architectural Press, forthcoming). Roger has taught and lectured widely, including Harvard University, Los Angeles' Zocalo Public Square, and New York's Museum of Modern Art.

ROCHELLE STEINER is the former dean of the Roski School of Fine Arts at the University of Southern California. She was the curator for the exhibition *6 Under 60*, part of the 2011 Hong Kong & Shenzhen Biennale of Urbanism/Architecture. Previously she was director of the Public Art Fund in New York (2006–09), where she commissioned 35 public art projects with established and emerging international artists, including Olafur Eliasson's *The New York City Waterfalls*. She served as chief curator at the Serpentine Gallery in London (2001–06), where she curated exhibitions with internationally acclaimed artists, including Ellsworth Kelly, Takashi Murakami, Gabriel Orozco, Cindy Sherman, and Rirkrit Tiravanija. In addition, she has held curatorial positions at the Saint Louis Art Museum and Walker Art Center. She has published more than 50 catalogues and essays on contemporary art and artists. Steiner holds a PhD in Visual and Cultural Studies from the University of Rochester.

MARK WASIUTA teaches at Columbia University where he is co-director of the CCCP in the architecture program. He is also Director of Exhibitions. Wasiuta is partner in the International House of Architecture. He is co-editor and co-author of the books "Dan Graham's New Jersey" as well as the forthcoming "Environments and Counter Environments," Experimental Media in *Italy: The New Domestic Landscape*."

ACKNOWLEDGMENTS
This book was produced with generous support from the University of Southern California School of Architecture and the Goethe Institut, Los Angeles. I am grateful for the encouragement of Gail Borden, Diane Ghirardo, Alice Kimm, Qingyun Ma, and Amy Murphy. The University of Southern California students who participated in the Urban States Workshop—Kimberly Bahnsen, Yin-Fun Chou, Kathleen Gmyrek, Tianlian Gu, Christina Hwang, Winston Kahn, Fallon Lebedowicz, Ben Marcus, Jennifer Renteria, Catherine Rilla and Xin Tong—are an essential part of this project. I would like to also thank Isabelle Chafkin and James Michael Tate for their input; Carlos Gutierrez and Regina Teng for their tireless assistance; Rene Daalder, Jerry Goren, Marcelyn Gow, William Mohline, Pascale Richter, John Southern, John C. Woell, and Mimi Zeiger for being the best of critics and friends. At home Alain Fièvre is always a beacon of inspiration and stability.

INFORMAL L.A.
The Space of Politics
Edited by Victor J. Jones

Design: Zak Group
Typeface: *Plain* by François Rappo
Copy Editing: Elizabeth Pulsinelli

Photography:
Reid Cigolle, front and back covers, inside covers, pages 8–9, 14–15, 22–23, 30–31, 40–41, 50–51, 58–59, 78–79, 92–93, 102–103, 118–19, 126–27

Logistics and Video Reporting:
Ian McCully, Raul Lopez, Gennaro Avolio Toly, Take One Productions

ISBN: 978-1-938740-04-6

Published by: eVolo

eVolo NY
570 W. 204th Street. 1B
New York, NY 10034 USA

eVolo LA
6363 Wilshire Blvd. 311
Los Angeles, CA 90048 USA

contact@evolo.us
www.evolo.us
Printed in China